INTRODUCTION TO
Python
Programming

By

Anthony Mc Fedden

TABLE OF CONTENTS

INTRODUCTION TO PYTHON PROGRAMMING

WHAT IS PYTHON?

The idea of Python originated in 1989 when its creator Guido van Rossum was confronted by the shortcomings of ABC language (namely extensibility). Rossum started work on developing a new language that integrated all good features of ABC language and new desired features, such as extensibility and exception handling. Python 1.0 was released in 1994; it borrowed the module system from Modula-3, had the capability to interact with Amoeba operating system, and included functional programming tools.

In 2000, Python's core development team moved to Beopen.com, and in October 2000, Python 2.0 was released with many improvisations including a garbage collector and support for Unicode.

December 2008 saw the release of Python 3.0, giving up backward compatibility and possessing a new design to avoid duplicative constructs and modules. It is still a multi-paradigm language offering developers the options of object-orientation, structured programming and functional programming.

Python today has multiple implementations including Jython, scripted in Java language for Java Virtual Machine; IronPython written in C# for the Common Language Infrastructure, and PyPy version written in RPython and translated into C. To be noted, Cpython which is written in C and developed by Python Software Foundation is the default and most popular implementation of Python. While these implementations work in the native language they are written in, they are also capable of interacting with other languages through use of modules. Most of these modules work on community development model and are open-source and free.

Released in February 2015, Python 3.4.3 offers drastic improvement in Unicode support, among other new features. Python 3.5 is currently in development, with scheduled release in September 2015.

Applications of Python

- GUI based desktop applications
- Image processing and graphic design applications
- Scientific and computational applications
- Games
- Web frameworks and web applications
- Enterprise and business applications
- Operating systems
- Language development
- Prototyping

Advantages/Benefits of Python

The diverse application of the Python language is a result of the combination of features which give this language an edge over others. Some of the benefits of programming in Python include:

1. Presence of Third Party Modules:

The Python Package Index (PyPI) contains numerous third-party modules that make Python capable of interacting with most of the other languages and platforms.

2. Extensive Support Libraries:

Python provides a large standard library which includes areas like internet protocols, string operations, web services tools and operating system interfaces. Many high use programming tasks have already been scripted into the standard library which reduces length of code to be written significantly.

3. Open Source and Community Development:

Python language is developed under an OSI-approved open source license, which makes it free to use and distribute, including for commercial purposes.

Further, its development is driven by the community which collaborates for its code through hosting conferences and mailing lists, and provides for its numerous modules.

4. Learning Ease and Support Available:

Python offers excellent readability and uncluttered simple-to-learn syntax which helps beginners to utilize this programming language. The code style guidelines, PEP 8, provide a set of rules to facilitate the formatting of code. Additionally, the wide base of users and active developers has resulted in a rich internet resource bank to encourage development and the continued adoption of the language.

5. User-friendly Data Structures:

Python has built-in list and dictionary data structures which can be used to construct fast runtime data structures. Further, Python also provides the option of dynamic high-level data typing which reduces the length of support code that is needed.

6. Productivity and Speed:

Python has clean object-oriented design, provides enhanced process control capabilities, and possesses strong integration and text processing capabilities and its own unit testing framework, all of which contribute to the increase in its speed and productivity. Python is considered a viable option for building complex multi-protocol network applications.

As can be seen from the above-mentioned points, Python offers a number of advantages for software development. As upgrading of the language continues, its loyalist base could grow as well.

7. It Is Free

Python is an open-source language. The Python company is one of the largest companies and, still, is free. Using python language doesn't require a particular subscription or a custom-built platform either, thus any desktop and laptop is compatible with Python. All the tools that are necessary for python coding, the supporting means, modules, and libraries are absolutely free.

The essential IDEs that is, the integrated development environments that include PTVS, Pydev with eclipse spyder python can be downloaded easily for free. Reduced costs are always beneficial to businesses.

8. It Needs Less Coding

Python by nature has a very simple syntax. The same logic that needs 7 lines in a C++ language, requires just 3 lines in Python. Having a smaller code requires less space, less time, and is well appreciated by coders, as the rework or correction also takes lesser time. The language aces all the parameters of readability. To support itself, the language has many built-ins and libraries that make it easy to comprehend.

Software that requires less time to code utilizes fewer resources and less time and, thus, helps in cost reduction and yields more profits.

9. All Kinds Of Businesses Can Afford It

Being a free platform, all small and medium level companies can use it. Companies that are in the nascent stage can use the python platform and begin their operations with cost-effective software. The ability to develop applications and software quickly makes it suitable for startups, as they can survive in the cutthroat competition by leveraging the speed of the python language.

10. Big Giants Are Using It

It is not only suitable for small-medium companies, but leading companies like Google, Spotify, Instagram, and Dropbox, also vouch for python development over other languages. NASA, Electronic Arts, and Disney are among the top non-IT giants who have migrated to the Python environment.

11. It Is One Of The Most Trending Languages

Java and C++ are the native languages with the Object Oriented approach. Their use is very widespread, and efficiency is tremendous. The only problem with these languages is they are lengthy. The codes are cumbersome and, thus, to correct or to rework is an immensely tedious process. Python, on the other hand, has all the features of object-oriented programming just like Java and C++, and is fast too. The codes are shorter and the syntax simple, thus being easy to amend, rework and optimize.

12. Python Is For Everyone Involved In Software Making

Every software product is the result of a series of software architecture that is built, a series of rigorous coding and testing. There is a lot of back and forth concerning matching the actual output with the desired output.

When a lot is working around the code, it is essential that the language the whole program is coded in is understood very well by everyone; from the developer to the tester and everyone in the middle. Python is a language that is suitable for everyone. Easy to comprehend and analyze.

A business depends on the software and its functionality, and the software depends on the way it is coded. Programming languages help you to build a well-coded software that will ultimately lead to a great company. Python is a language that would make great software. Python has all the features that make it a true language that is accepted and appreciated all around the globe.

Python is available on a wide variety of platforms including Linux and Mac OS X. Let's understand how to set up our Python environment.

LOCAL ENVIRONMENT SETUP

Open a terminal window and type "python" to find out if it is already installed and which version is installed.

- Unix (Solaris, Linux, FreeBSD, AIX, HP/UX, SunOS, IRIX, etc.)
- Win 9x/NT/2000
- Macintosh (Intel, PPC, 68K)
- OS/2
- DOS (multiple versions)
- PalmOS
- Nokia mobile phones
- Windows CE
- Acorn/RISC OS
- BeOS
- Amiga
- VMS/OpenVMS
- QNX
- VxWorks
- Psion
- Python has also been ported to the Java and .NET virtual machines

GETTING PYTHON

The most up-to-date and current source code, binaries, documentation, news, etc., is available on the official website of Python https://www.python.org/

You can download Python documentation from https://www.python.org/doc/. The documentation is available in HTML, PDF, and PostScript formats.

INSTALLING PYTHON

Python distribution is available for a wide variety of platforms. You need to download only the binary code applicable for your platform and install Python.

If the binary code for your platform is not available, you need a C compiler to compile the source code manually. Compiling the source code offers more flexibility in terms of choice of features that you require in your installation.

Here is a quick overview of installing Python on various platforms –

Unix and Linux Installation

Here are the simple steps to install Python on Unix/Linux machine.

- Open a Web browser and go to https://www.python.org/downloads/.

- Follow the link to download zipped source code available for Unix/Linux.

- Download and extract files.

- Editing the Modules/Setup file if you want to customize some options.

- run ./configure script

- make

- make install

This installs Python at standard location /usr/local/bin and its libraries at /usr/local/lib/pythonXX where XX is the version of Python.

Windows Installation

Here are the steps to install Python on Windows machine.

- Open a Web browser and go to https://www.python.org/downloads/.

- Follow the link for the Windows installer python-XYZ.msi file where XYZ is the version you need to install.

- To use this installer python-XYZ.msi, the Windows system must support Microsoft Installer 2.0. Save the installer file to your local machine and then run it to find out if your machine supports MSI.

- Run the downloaded file. This brings up the Python install wizard, which is really easy to use. Just accept the default settings, wait until the install is finished, and you are done.

Macintosh Installation

Recent Macs come with Python installed, but it may be several years out of date. See http://www.python.org/download/mac/ for instructions on getting the current version along with extra tools to support development on the Mac. For older Mac OS's before Mac OS X 10.3 (released in 2003), MacPython is available.

Jack Jansen maintains it and you can have full access to the entire documentation at his website – http://www.cwi.nl/~jack/macpython.html. You can find complete installation details for Mac OS installation.

Setting up PATH

Programs and other executable files can be in many directories, so operating systems provide a search path that lists the directories that the OS searches for executables.

The path is stored in an environment variable, which is a named string maintained by the operating system. This variable contains information available to the command shell and other programs.

The path variable is named as PATH in Unix or Path in Windows (Unix is case sensitive; Windows is not).

In Mac OS, the installer handles the path details. To invoke the Python interpreter from any particular directory, you must add the Python directory to your path.

Setting path at Unix/Linux

To add the Python directory to the path for a particular session in Unix –

- In the csh shell – type setenv PATH "$PATH:/usr/local/bin/python" and press Enter.

- In the bash shell (Linux) – type export PATH="$PATH:/usr/local/bin/python" and press Enter.

- In the sh or ksh shell – type PATH="$PATH:/usr/local/bin/python" and press Enter.

- Note – /usr/local/bin/python is the path of the Python directory

Setting path at Windows

To add the Python directory to the path for a particular session in Windows –

At   the   **command   prompt**   –   type   path %path%;C:\Python and press Enter.

Note – C:\Python is the path of the Python directory

Python Environment Variables

Here are important environment variables, which can be recognized by Python –

Sr.No.	Variable & Description
1	**PYTHONPATH** It has a role similar to PATH. This variable tells the Python interpreter where to locate the module files imported into a program. It should include the Python source library directory and the directories containing Python source code. PYTHONPATH is sometimes preset by the Python installer.
2	**PYTHONSTARTUP** It contains the path of an initialization file containing Python source code. It is executed every time you start the interpreter. It is named as .pythonrc.py in Unix and it contains commands that load utilities or modify PYTHONPATH.
3	**PYTHONCASEOK** It is used in Windows to instruct Python to find the first case-insensitive match in an import statement. Set this variable to any value to activate it.
4	**PYTHONHOME** It is an alternative module search path. It is usually embedded in the PYTHONSTARTUP or PYTHONPATH directories to make switching module libraries easy.

RUNNING PYTHON

There are three different ways to start Python –

Interactive Interpreter

You can start Python from Unix, DOS, or any other system that provides you a command-line interpreter or shell window.

Enter python the command line.

Start coding right away in the interactive interpreter.

```
$python # Unix/Linux

or

python% # Unix/Linux

or

C:> python # Windows/DOS
```

Here is the list of all the available command line options –

Sr.No.	Option & Description
1	**-d** It provides debug output.
2	**-O** It generates optimized bytecode (resulting in .pyo files).

| 3 | **-S** |
| | Do not run import site to look for Python paths on startup. |

| 4 | **-v** |
| | verbose output (detailed trace on import statements). |

| 5 | **-X** |
| | disable class-based built-in exceptions (just use strings); obsolete starting with version 1.6. |

| 6 | **-c cmd** |
| | run Python script sent in as cmd string |

| 7 | **file** |
| | run Python script from given file |

Script from the Command-line

A Python script can be executed at command line by invoking the interpreter on your application, as in the following-

```
$python script.py # Unix/Linux
```

or

```
python% script.py # Unix/Linux

or

C: >python script.py # Windows/DOS
```

Note – Be sure the file permission mode allows execution.

Integrated Development Environment

You can run Python from a Graphical User Interface (GUI) environment as well, if you have a GUI application on your system that supports Python.

- **Unix** – IDLE is the very first Unix IDE for Python.

- **Windows** – PythonWin is the first Windows interface for Python and is an IDE with a GUI.

- **Macintosh** – The Macintosh version of Python along with the IDLE IDE is available from the main website, downloadable as either MacBinary or BinHex'd files.

If you are not able to set up the environment properly, then you can take help from your system admin. Make sure the Python environment is properly set up and working perfectly fine.

Note – All the examples given in subsequent chapters are executed with Python 2.4.3 version available on CentOS flavor of Linux.

We already have set up Python Programming environment online, so that you can execute all the available examples online at the same time when you are learning theory. Feel free to modify any example and execute it online.

The Python language has many similarities to Perl, C, and Java. However, there are some definite differences between the languages.

FIRST PYTHON
PROGRAM

Let us execute programs in different modes of programming.

Interactive Mode Programming

Invoking the interpreter without passing a script file as a parameter brings up the following prompt –

```
$ python

Python 2.4.3 (#1, Nov 11 2010, 13:34:43)

[GCC 4.1.2 20080704 (Red Hat 4.1.2-48)] on linux2

Type "help", "copyright", "credits" or "license" for more information.

>>>
```

Type the following text at the Python prompt and press the Enter –

```
>>> print "Hello, Python!"
```

If you are running new version of Python, then you would need to use print statement with parenthesis as in print ("Hello, Python!");. However in Python version 2.4.3, this produces the following result –

```
Hello, Python!
```

Script Mode Programming

Invoking the interpreter with a script parameter begins execution of the script and continues until the script is finished. When the script is finished, the interpreter is no longer active.

Let us write a simple Python program in a script. Python files have extension **.py**. Type the following source code in a test.py file –

```
print "Hello, Python!"
```

We assume that you have Python interpreter set in PATH variable. Now, try to run this program as follows –

```
$ python test.py
```

This produces the following result –

```
Hello, Python!
```

Let us try another way to execute a Python script. Here is the modified test.py file –

```
#!/usr/bin/python

print "Hello, Python!"
```

We assume that you have Python interpreter available in /usr/bin directory. Now, try to run this program as follows –

```
$ chmod +x test.py     # This is to make file executable

$./test.py
```

This produces the following result –

```
Hello, Python!
```

PYTHON IDENTIFIERS

A Python identifier is a name used to identify a variable, function, class, module or other object. An identifier starts with a letter A to Z or a to z or an underscore (_) followed by zero or more letters, underscores and digits (0 to 9).

Python does not allow punctuation characters such as @, $, and % within identifiers. Python is a case sensitive programming language. Thus, **Manpower** and **manpower** are two different identifiers in Python.

Here are naming conventions for Python identifiers –

- Class names start with an uppercase letter. All other identifiers start with a lowercase letter.

- Starting an identifier with a single leading underscore indicates that the identifier is private.

- Starting an identifier with two leading underscores indicates a strongly private identifier.

- If the identifier also ends with two trailing underscores, the identifier is a language-defined special name.

RESERVED WORDS

The following list shows the Python keywords. These are reserved words and you cannot use them as constant or variable or any other identifier names. All the Python keywords contain lowercase letters only.

And	exec	not
Assert	finally	or
Break	for	pass
Class	from	print
Continue	global	raise
Def	if	return
Del	import	try
Elif	in	while
Else	is	with
Except	lambda	yield

LINES AND INDENTATION

Python provides no braces to indicate blocks of code for class and function definitions or flow control. Blocks of code are denoted by line indentation, which is rigidly enforced.

The number of spaces in the indentation is variable, but all statements within the block must be indented the same amount. For example –

```
if True:
   print "True"
else:
   print "False"
```

However, the following block generates an error –

```
if True:
print "Answer"
print "True"
else:
print "Answer"
print "False"
```

Thus, in Python all the continuous lines indented with same number of spaces would form a block. The following example has various statement blocks –

Note – Do not try to understand the logic at this point of time. Just make sure you understood various blocks even if they are without braces.

```python
#!/usr/bin/python
import sys
try:
    # open file stream
    file = open(file_name, "w")
except IOError:
    print "There was an error writing to", file_name
    sys.exit()
print "Enter '", file_finish,
print "' When finished"
while file_text != file_finish:
    file_text = raw_input("Enter text: ")
    if file_text == file_finish:
        # close the file
        file.close
        break
    file.write(file_text)
    file.write("\n")
file.close()
file_name = raw_input("Enter filename: ")
if len(file_name) == 0:
    print "Next time please enter something"
    sys.exit()
try:
    file = open(file_name, "r")
except IOError:
```

```
    print "There was an error reading file"

    sys.exit()
file_text = file.read()
file.close()
print file_text
```

MULTI-LINE STATEMENTS

Statements in Python typically end with a new line. Python does, however, allow the use of the line continuation character (\) to denote that the line should continue. For example –

```
total = item_one + \

    item_two + \

    item_three
```

Statements contained within the [], {, or () brackets do not need to use the line continuation character. For example –

```
days = ['Monday', 'Tuesday', 'Wednesday',

    'Thursday', 'Friday']
```

QUOTATION IN PYTHON

Python accepts single ('), double (") and triple (''' or """) quotes to denote string literals, as long as the same type of quote starts and ends the string.

The triple quotes are used to span the string across multiple lines. For example, all the following are legal –

```
word = 'word'

sentence = "This is a sentence."

paragraph = """This is a paragraph. It is

made up of multiple lines and sentences."""
```

Comments in Python

A hash sign (#) that is not inside a string literal begins a comment. All characters after the # and up to the end of the physical line are part of the comment and the Python interpreter ignores them.

```
#!/usr/bin/python


# First comment

print "Hello, Python!" # second comment
```

This produces the result:

```
Hello, Python!
```

You can type a comment on the same line after a statement or expression –

```
name = "Madisetti" # This is again comment
```

You can comment multiple lines as follows –

```
# This is a comment.

# This is a comment, too.

# This is a comment, too.
```

```
# I said that already.
```

Following triple-quoted string is also ignored by Python interpreter and can be used as a multiline comments:

```
'''
This is a multiline
comment.
'''
```

Using Blank Lines

A line containing only whitespace, possibly with a comment, is known as a blank line and Python totally ignores it.

In an interactive interpreter session, you must enter an empty physical line to terminate a multiline statement.

Waiting for the User

The following line of the program displays the prompt, the statement saying "Press the enter key to exit", and waits for the user to take action –

```
#!/usr/bin/python

raw_input("\n\nPress the enter key to exit.")
```

Here, "\n\n" is used to create two new lines before displaying the actual line. Once the user presses the key, the program ends. This is a nice trick to keep a console window open until the user is done with an application.

Multiple Statements on a Single Line

The semicolon (;) allows multiple statements on the single line given that neither statement starts a new code block. Here is a sample snip using the semicolon –

```
import sys; x = 'foo'; sys.stdout.write(x + '\n')
```

Multiple Statement Groups as Suites

A group of individual statements, which make a single code block are called suites in Python. Compound or complex statements, such as if, while, def, and class require a header line and a suite.

Header lines begin the statement (with the keyword) and terminate with a colon (:) and are followed by one or more lines which make up the suite. For example –

```
if expression :
    suite
elif expression :
    suite
else :
    suite
```

Command Line Arguments

Many programs can be run to provide you with some basic information about how they should be run. Python enables you to do this with -h –

```
$ python -h

usage: python [option] ... [-c cmd | -m mod | file | -] [arg] ...

Options and arguments (and corresponding environment variables):

-c cmd : program passed in as string (terminates option list)

-d     : debug output from parser (also PYTHONDEBUG=x)

-E     : ignore environment variables (such as PYTHONPATH)

-h     : print this help message and exit


[ etc. ]
```

You can also program your script in such a way that it should accept various options. Command Line Arguments is an advanced topic and should be studied a bit later once you have gone through rest of the Python concepts.

Variables are nothing but reserved memory locations to store values. This means that when you create a variable you reserve some space in memory.

Based on the data type of a variable, the interpreter allocates memory and decides what can be stored in the reserved memory. Therefore, by assigning different data types to variables, you can store integers, decimals or characters in these variables.

Assigning Values to Variables

Python variables do not need explicit declaration to reserve memory space. The declaration happens automatically when you assign a value to a variable. The equal sign (=) is used to assign values to variables.

The operand to the left of the = operator is the name of the variable and the operand to the right of the = operator is the value stored in the variable. For example –

```
#!/usr/bin/python


counter = 100        # An integer assignment

miles   = 1000.0     # A floating point

name    = "John"     # A string


print counter

print miles

print name
```

Here, 100, 1000.0 and "John" are the values assigned to counter, miles, and name variables, respectively. This produces the following result –

```
100
1000.0
John
```

Multiple Assignment

Python allows you to assign a single value to several variables simultaneously. For example –

```
a = b = c = 1
```

Here, an integer object is created with the value 1, and all three variables are assigned to the same memory location. You can also assign multiple objects to multiple variables. For example –

```
a,b,c = 1,2,"john"
```

Here, two integer objects with values 1 and 2 are assigned to variables a and b respectively, and one string object with the value "john" is assigned to the variable c.

Standard Data Types

The data stored in memory can be of many types. For example, a person's age is stored as a numeric value and his or her address is stored as alphanumeric characters. Python has various standard data types that are used to define the operations possible on them and the storage method for each of them.

Python has five standard data types –

- Numbers
- String
- List
- Tuple
- Dictionary

PYTHON NUMBERS

Number data types store numeric values. Number objects are created when you assign a value to them. For example –

```
var1 = 1
var2 = 10
```

You can also delete the reference to a number object by using the del statement. The syntax of the del statement is –

```
del var1[,var2[,var3[....,varN]]]]
```

You can delete a single object or multiple objects by using the del statement. For example –

```
del var
del var_a, var_b
```

Python supports four different numerical types –

- int (signed integers)
- long (long integers, they can also be represented in octal and hexadecimal)
- float (floating point real values)
- complex (complex numbers)

Examples

int	Long	float	complex
10	51924361L	0.0	3.14j
100	-0x19323L	15.20	45.j
-786	0122L	-21.9	9.322e-36j
080	0xDEFABCECBDAE CBFBAEl	32.3+e 18	.876j
-0490	535633629843L	-90.	-.6545+0J
- 0x260	-052318172735L	- 32.54e 100	3e+26J
0x69	-4721885298529L	70.2- E12	4.53e-7j
int	Long	float	complex

10	51924361L	0.0	3.14j
100	-0x19323L	15.20	45.j
-786	0122L	-21.9	9.322e-36j
080	0xDEFABCECBDAE CBFBAEl	32.3+e 18	.876j
-0490	535633629843L	-90.	-.6545+0J
- 0x260	-052318172735L	- 32.54e 100	3e+26J
0x69	-4721885298529L	70.2- E12	4.53e-7j

Here are some examples of numbers –

- Python allows you to use a lowercase l with long, but it is recommended that you use only an uppercase L to avoid confusion with the number 1. Python displays long integers with an uppercase L.

- A complex number consists of an ordered pair of real floating-point numbers denoted by x + yj, where x and y are the real numbers and j is the imaginary unit.

PYTHON STRINGS

Strings in Python are identified as a contiguous set of characters represented in the quotation marks. Python allows for either pairs of single or double quotes. Subsets of strings can be taken using the slice operator ([ ] and [:]) with indexes starting at 0 in the beginning of the string and working their way from -1 at the end.

The plus (+) sign is the string concatenation operator and the asterisk (*) is the repetition operator. For example –

```
#!/usr/bin/python


str = 'Hello World!'


print str          # Prints complete string

print str[0]       # Prints first character of the string

print str[2:5]     # Prints characters starting from 3rd to 5th

print str[2:]      # Prints string starting from 3rd character

print str * 2      # Prints string two times

print str + "TEST" # Prints concatenated string
```

This will produce the following result −

```
Hello World!

H

llo

llo World!

Hello World!Hello World!

Hello World!TEST
```

Python Lists

Lists are the most versatile of Python's compound data types. A list contains items separated by commas and enclosed within square brackets ([]). To some extent, lists are similar to arrays in C. One difference between them is that all the items belonging to a list can be of different data type.

The values stored in a list can be accessed using the slice operator ([ ] and [:]) with indexes starting at 0 in the beginning of the list and working their way to end - 1. The plus (+) sign is the list concatenation operator, and the asterisk (*) is the repetition operator. For example −

```
#!/usr/bin/python


list = [ 'abcd', 786 , 2.23, 'john', 70.2 ]

tinylist = [123, 'john']


print list        # Prints complete list
```

```
print list[0]      # Prints first element of the list

print list[1:3]     # Prints elements starting from 2nd till 3rd

print list[2:]      # Prints elements starting from 3rd element

print tinylist * 2  # Prints list two times

print list + tinylist # Prints concatenated lists
```

This produce the following result −

```
['abcd', 786, 2.23, 'john', 70.2]

abcd

[786, 2.23]

[2.23, 'john', 70.2]

[123, 'john', 123, 'john']

['abcd', 786, 2.23, 'john', 70.2, 123, 'john']
```

Python Tuples

A tuple is another sequence data type that is similar to the list. A tuple consists of a number of values separated by commas. Unlike lists, however, tuples are enclosed within parentheses.

The main differences between lists and tuples are: Lists are enclosed in brackets ([ ]) and their elements and size can be changed, while tuples are enclosed in parentheses (( )) and cannot be updated. Tuples can be thought of as read-only lists. For example −

```
#!/usr/bin/python

tuple = ( 'abcd', 786 , 2.23, 'john', 70.2  )
tinytuple = (123, 'john')

print tuple          # Prints complete list
print tuple[0]       # Prints first element of the list
print tuple[1:3]     # Prints elements starting from 2nd till 3rd
print tuple[2:]      # Prints elements starting from 3rd element
print tinytuple * 2  # Prints list two times
print tuple + tinytuple # Prints concatenated lists
```

This produce the following result –

```
('abcd', 786, 2.23, 'john', 70.2)
abcd
(786, 2.23)
(2.23, 'john', 70.2)
(123, 'john', 123, 'john')
('abcd', 786, 2.23, 'john', 70.2, 123, 'john')
```

The following code is invalid with tuple, because we attempted to update a tuple, which is not allowed. Similar case is possible with lists –

```
#!/usr/bin/python


tuple = ( 'abcd', 786 , 2.23, 'john', 70.2 )

list = [ 'abcd', 786 , 2.23, 'john', 70.2 ]

tuple[2] = 1000    # Invalid syntax with tuple

list[2] = 1000    # Valid syntax with list
```

PYTHON DICTIONARY

Python's dictionaries are kind of hash table type. They work like associative arrays or hashes found in Perl and consist of key-value pairs. A dictionary key can be almost any Python type, but are usually numbers or strings. Values, on the other hand, can be any arbitrary Python object.

Dictionaries are enclosed by curly braces ({}) and values can be assigned and accessed using square braces ([]). For example –

```
#!/usr/bin/python


dict = {}

dict['one'] = "This is one"

dict[2]     = "This is two"


tinydict = {'name': 'john','code':6734, 'dept': 'sales'}


print dict['one']      # Prints value for 'one' key

print dict[2]          # Prints value for 2 key

print tinydict         # Prints complete dictionary

print tinydict.keys()   # Prints all the keys

print tinydict.values() # Prints all the values
```

This produce the following result –

```
This is one

This is two

{'dept': 'sales', 'code': 6734, 'name': 'john'}

['dept', 'code', 'name']

['sales', 6734, 'john']
```

Dictionaries have no concept of order among elements. It is incorrect to say that the elements are "out of order"; they are simply unordered.

Data Type Conversion

Sometimes, you may need to perform conversions between the built-in types. To convert between types, you simply use the type name as a function.

There are several built-in functions to perform conversion from one data type to another. These functions return a new object representing the converted value.

Sr.No.	Function & Description
1	**int(x [,base])** Converts x to an integer. base specifies the base if x is a string.
2	**long(x [,base])** Converts x to a long integer. base specifies the base if x is a string.

3	**float(x)**
	Converts x to a floating-point number.

4	**complex(real [,imag])**
	Creates a complex number.

5	**str(x)**
	Converts object x to a string representation.

6	**repr(x)**
	Converts object x to an expression string.

7	**eval(str)**
	Evaluates a string and returns an object.

8	**tuple(s)**
	Converts s to a tuple.

9	**list(s)**
	Converts s to a list.

10	**set(s)**
	Converts s to a set.

11   **dict(d)**

Creates a dictionary. d must be a sequence of (key,value) tuples.

12   **frozenset(s)**

Converts s to a frozen set.

13   **chr(x)**

Converts an integer to a character.

14   **unichr(x)**

Converts an integer to a Unicode character.

15   **ord(x)**

Converts a single character to its integer value.

16   **hex(x)**

Converts an integer to a hexadecimal string.

17   **oct(x)**

Converts an integer to an octal string.

OPERATORS

Operators are the constructs which can manipulate the value of operands.

Consider the expression 4 + 5 = 9. Here, 4 and 5 are called operands and + is called operator.

Types of Operator

Python language supports the following types of operators.

- Arithmetic Operators
- Comparison (Relational) Operators
- Assignment Operators
- Logical Operators
- Bitwise Operators
- Membership Operators
- Identity Operators

Let us have a look on all operators one by one.

Python Arithmetic Operators

Assume variable a holds 10 and variable b holds 20, then –

Operator	Description	Example
+ Addition	Adds values on either side of the operator.	a + b = 30
- Subtraction	Subtracts right hand operand from left hand operand.	a – b = -10
* Multiplication	Multiplies values on either side of the operator	a * b = 200
/ Division	Divides left hand operand by right hand operand	b / a = 2
% Modulus	Divides left hand operand by right hand operand and returns remainder	b % a = 0

** Exponent	Performs exponential (power) calculation on operators	a**b =10 to the power 20
//	Floor Division - The division of operands where the result is the quotient in which the digits after the decimal point are removed. But if one of the operands is negative, the result is floored, i.e., rounded away from zero (towards negative infinity) –	9//2 = 4 and 9.0//2.0 = 4.0, -11//3 = -4, -11.0//3 = -4.0

Python Comparison Operators

These operators compare the values on either sides of them and decide the relation among them. They are also called Relational operators.

Assume variable a holds 10 and variable b holds 20, then –

Operator	Description	Example
==	If the values of two operands are equal,	(a == b) is not true.

	then the condition becomes true.	
!=	If values of two operands are not equal, then condition becomes true.	(a != b) is true.
<>	If values of two operands are not equal, then condition becomes true.	(a <> b) is true. This is similar to != operator.
>	If the value of left operand is greater than the value of right operand, then condition becomes true.	(a > b) is not true.
<	If the value of left operand is less than the value of right operand, then condition becomes true.	(a < b) is true.
>=	If the value of left operand is greater than or equal to the	(a >= b) is not true.

Operator	Description	Example
	value of right operand, then condition becomes true.	
<=	If the value of left operand is less than or equal to the value of right operand, then condition becomes true.	(a <= b) is true.

Python Assignment Operators

Assume variable a holds 10 and variable b holds 20, then –

Operator	Description	Example
=	Assigns values from right side operands to left side operand	c = a + b assigns value of a + b into c
+= Add AND	It adds right operand to the left operand and assign the result to left operand	c += a is equivalent to c = c + a

-= Subtract AND	It subtracts right operand from the left operand and assign the result to left operand	c -= a is equivalent to c = c - a
*= Multiply AND	It multiplies right operand with the left operand and assign the result to left operand	c *= a is equivalent to c = c * a
/= Divide AND	It divides left operand with the right operand and assign the result to left operand	c /= a is equivalent to c = c / ac /= a is equivalent to c = c / a
%= Modulus AND	It takes modulus using two operands and assign the result to left operand	c %= a is equivalent to c = c % a
**= Exponent AND	Performs exponential (power) calculation on operators and	c **= a is equivalent to c = c ** a

	assign value to the left operand	
//= Floor Division	It performs floor division on operators and assign value to the left operand	c //= a is equivalent to c = c // a

Python Bitwise Operators

Bitwise operator works on bits and performs bit by bit operation. Assume if a = 60; and b = 13; Now in binary format they will be as follows −

a = 0011 1100

b = 0000 1101

----

a&b = 0000 1100

a|b = 0011 1101

a^b = 0011 0001

~a = 1100 0011

There are following Bitwise operators supported by Python language

Operator	Description	Example
& Binary AND	Operator copies a bit to the result if it exists in both operands	(a & b) (means 0000 1100)
| Binary OR	It copies a bit if it exists in either operand.	(a | b) = 61 (means 0011 1101)
^ Binary XOR	It copies the bit if it is set in one operand but not both.	(a ^ b) = 49 (means 0011 0001)
~ Binary Ones Complement	It is unary and has the effect of 'flipping' bits.	(~a) = -61 (means 1100 0011 in 2's complement form due to a signed binary number.
<< Binary Left Shift	The left operands value is moved left by the number of	a << 2 = 240 (means 1111 0000)

	bits specified by the right operand.	
>> Binary Right Shift	The left operands value is moved right by the number of bits specified by the right operand.	a >> 2 = 15 (means 0000 1111)

Python Logical Operators

There are following logical operators supported by Python language. Assume variable a holds 10 and variable b holds 20 then

Operator	Description	Example
and Logical AND	If both the operands are true then condition becomes true.	(a and b) is true.
or Logical OR	If any of the two operands are non-zero then condition becomes true.	(a or b) is true.

not Logical NOT	Used to reverse the logical state of its operand.	Not(a and b) is false.

Used to reverse the logical state of its operand.

Python Membership Operators

Python's membership operators test for membership in a sequence, such as strings, lists, or tuples. There are two membership operators as explained below –

Operator	Description	Example
in	Evaluates to true if it finds a variable in the specified sequence and false otherwise.	x in y, here in results in a 1 if x is a member of sequence y.
not in	Evaluates to true if it does not finds a variable in the specified sequence and false otherwise.	x not in y, here not in results in a 1 if x is not a member of sequence y.

Python Identity Operators

Identity operators compare the memory locations of two objects. There are two Identity operators explained below −

Operator	Description	Example
is	Evaluates to true if the variables on either side of the operator point to the same object and false otherwise.	x is y, here **is** results in 1 if id(x) equals id(y).
is not	Evaluates to false if the variables on either side of the operator point to the same object and true otherwise.	x is not y, here **is not** results in 1 if id(x) is not equal to id(y).

Python Operators Precedence

The following table lists all operators from highest precedence to lowest.

Sr.No.	Operator & Description
1	** Exponentiation (raise to the power)
2	~ + - Complement, unary plus and minus (method names for the last two are +@ and -@)
3	* / % // Multiply, divide, modulo and floor division
4	+ - Addition and subtraction
5	>> << Right and left bitwise shift
6	& Bitwise 'AND'

7	^ |
	Bitwise exclusive `OR' and regular `OR'

8	<= < > >=
	Comparison operators

9	<> == !=
	Equality operators

10	= %= /= //= -= += *= **=
	Assignment operators

11	**is is not**
	Identity operators

12	**in not in**
	Membership operators

13	**not or and**
	Logical operators

CONDITIONAL STATEMENTS AND LOOPS

Decision making is anticipation of conditions occurring while execution of the program and specifying actions taken according to the conditions.

Decision structures evaluate multiple expressions which produce TRUE or FALSE as outcome. You need to determine which action to take and which statements to execute if outcome is TRUE or FALSE otherwise.

Following is the general form of a typical decision making structure found in most of the programming languages –

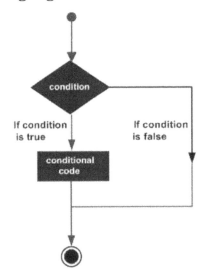

Python programming language assumes any non-zero and non-null values as TRUE, and if it is either zero or null, then it is assumed as FALSE value.

Python programming language provides following types of decision making statements. Click the following links to check their detail.

Sr.No.	Statement & Description
1	**if statements** An **if statement** consists of a boolean expression followed by one or more statements.
2	**if...else statements** An **if statement** can be followed by an optional **else statement**, which executes when the boolean expression is FALSE.
3	**nested if statements** You can use one **if** or **else if** statement inside another **if** or **else if**statement(s).

Let us go through each decision making briefly −

Single Statement Suites

If the suite of an if clause consists only of a single line, it may go on the same line as the header statement.

Here is an example of a one-line if clause −

```
#!/usr/bin/python


var = 100

if ( var == 100 ) : print "Value of expression is 100"

print "Good bye!"
```

When the above code is executed, it produces the following result –

```
Value of expression is 100

Good bye!
```

In general, statements are executed sequentially: The first statement in a function is executed first, followed by the second, and so on. There may be a situation when you need to execute a block of code several number of times.

Programming languages provide various control structures that allow for more complicated execution paths.

A loop statement allows us to execute a statement or group of statements multiple times. The following diagram illustrates a loop statement –

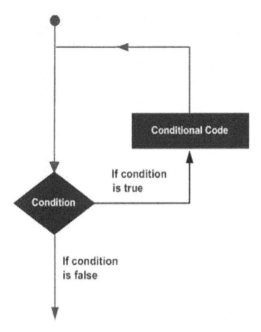

Python programming language provides following types of loops to handle looping requirements.

Sr.No.	Loop Type & Description
1	**while loop** Repeats a statement or group of statements while a given condition is TRUE. It tests the condition before executing the loop body.
2	**for loop** Executes a sequence of statements multiple times and abbreviates the code that manages the loop variable.

3	**nested loops**
	You can use one or more loop inside any another while, for or do..while loop.

Loop Control Statements

Loop control statements change execution from its normal sequence. When execution leaves a scope, all automatic objects that were created in that scope are destroyed.

Python supports the following control statements. Click the following links to check their detail.

Let us go through the loop control statements briefly

Sr.No.	Control Statement & Description
1	**break statement**
	Terminates the loop statement and transfers execution to the statement immediately following the loop.
2	**continue statement**
	Causes the loop to skip the remainder of its body and immediately retest its condition prior to reiterating.

3   **pass statement**

The pass statement in Python is used when a statement is required syntactically but you do not want any command or code to execute.

Number data types store numeric values. They are immutable data types, means that changing the value of a number data type results in a newly allocated object.

Number objects are created when you assign a value to them. For example –

```
var1 = 1
var2 = 10
```

You can also delete the reference to a number object by using the delstatement. The syntax of the del statement is –

```
del var1[,var2[,var3[....,varN]]]
```

You can delete a single object or multiple objects by using the del statement. For example –

```
del var
del var_a, var_b
```

Python supports four different numerical types –

- int (signed integers) – They are often called just integers or ints, are positive or negative whole numbers with no decimal point.

- long (long integers) – Also called longs, they are integers of unlimited size, written like integers and followed by an uppercase or lowercase L.

- float (floating point real values) – Also called floats, they represent real numbers and are written with a decimal point dividing the integer and fractional parts. Floats may also be in scientific notation, with E or e indicating the power of 10 (2.5e2 = 2.5 x 102 = 250).

- complex (complex numbers) – are of the form a + bJ, where a and b are floats and J (or j) represents the square root of -1 (which is an imaginary number). The real part of the number is a, and the imaginary part is b. Complex numbers are not used much in Python programming.

Examples

Here are some examples of numbers

int	Long	float	complex
10	51924361L	0.0	3.14j
100	-0x19323L	15.20	45.j
-786	0122L	-21.9	9.322e-36j

080	0Xdefabcecbdaecbfbael	32.3+e18	.876j
-0490	535633629843L	-90.	-.6545+0J
- 0x260	-052318172735L	- 32.54e100	3e+26J
0x69	-4721885298529L	70.2-E12	4.53e-7j

- Python allows you to use a lowercase L with long, but it is recommended that you use only an uppercase L to avoid confusion with the number 1. Python displays long integers with an uppercase L.

- A complex number consists of an ordered pair of real floating point numbers denoted by a + bj, where a is the real part and b is the imaginary part of the complex number.

Number Type Conversion

Python converts numbers internally in an expression containing mixed types to a common type for evaluation. But sometimes, you need to coerce a number explicitly from one type to another to satisfy the requirements of an operator or function parameter.

- Type int(x) to convert x to a plain integer.

- Type long(x) to convert x to a long integer.

- Type float(x) to convert x to a floating-point number.

- Type complex(x) to convert x to a complex number with real part x and imaginary part zero.

- Type complex(x, y) to convert x and y to a complex number with real part x and imaginary part y. x and y are numeric expressions

Mathematical Functions

Python includes following functions that perform mathematical calculations.

Sr.No.	Function & Returns (description)
1	**abs(x)** The absolute value of x: the (positive) distance between x and zero.
2	**ceil(x)** The ceiling of x: the smallest integer not less than x
3	**cmp(x, y)** -1 if x < y, 0 if x == y, or 1 if x > y
4	**exp(x)** The exponential of x: e^x

5   **fabs(x)**

The absolute value of x.

6   **floor(x)**

The floor of x: the largest integer not greater than x

7   **log(x)**

The natural logarithm of x, for x> 0

8   **log10(x)**

The base-10 logarithm of x for x> 0.

9   **max(x1, x2,...)**

The largest of its arguments: the value closest to positive infinity

10   **min(x1, x2,...)**

The smallest of its arguments: the value closest to negative infinity

11   **modf(x)**

The fractional and integer parts of x in a two-item tuple. Both parts have the same sign as x. The integer part is returned as a float.

12   **pow(x, y)**

The value of x**y.

13   **round(x [,n])**

x rounded to n digits from the decimal point.
Python rounds away from zero as a tie-breaker:
round(0.5) is 1.0 and round(-0.5) is -1.0.

14   **sqrt(x)**

The square root of x for x > 0

Random Number Functions

Random numbers are used for games, simulations,
testing, security, and privacy applications. Python
includes following functions that are commonly used.

Sr.No.	Function & Description

1   **choice(seq)**

A random item from a list, tuple, or string.

2   **randrange ([start,] stop [,step])**

A randomly selected element from range(start,
stop, step)

3	**random()**
	A random float r, such that 0 is less than or equal to r and r is less than 1
4	**seed([x])**
	Sets the integer starting value used in generating random numbers. Call this function before calling any other random module function. Returns None.
5	**shuffle(lst)**
	Randomizes the items of a list in place. Returns None.
6	**uniform(x, y)**
	A random float r, such that x is less than or equal to r and r is less than y

Trigonometric Functions

Python includes following functions that perform trigonometric calculations.

Sr.No.	Function & Description
1	**acos(x)**
	Return the arc cosine of x, in radians.

2   **asin(x)**

Return the arc sine of x, in radians.

3   **atan(x)**

Return the arc tangent of x, in radians.

4   **atan2(y, x)**

Return atan(y / x), in radians.

5   **cos(x)**

Return the cosine of x radians.

6   **hypot(x, y)**

Return the Euclidean norm, sqrt(x*x + y*y).

7   **sin(x)**

Return the sine of x radians.

8   **tan(x)**

Return the tangent of x radians.

9   **degrees(x)**

Converts angle x from radians to degrees.

10	**radians(x)**
	Converts angle x from degrees to radians.

Mathematical Constants

The module also defines two mathematical constants –

Sr.No.	Constants & Description
1	**Pi**
	The mathematical constant pi.
2	**E**
	The mathematical constant e.

Strings are amongst the most popular types in Python. We can create them simply by enclosing characters in quotes. Python treats single quotes the same as double quotes. Creating strings is as simple as assigning a value to a variable. For example –

```
var1 = 'Hello World!'

var2 = "Python Programming"
```

STRINGS

Python does not support a character type; these are treated as strings of length one, thus also considered a substring.

To access substrings, use the square brackets for slicing along with the index or indices to obtain your substring. For example –

```
#!/usr/bin/python


var1 = 'Hello World!'

var2 = "Python Programming"


print "var1[0]: ", var1[0]

print "var2[1:5]: ", var2[1:5]
```

When the above code is executed, it produces the following result –

```
var1[0]:  H
var2[1:5]:  ytho
```

Updating Strings

You can "update" an existing string by (re)assigning a variable to another string. The new value can be related to its previous value or to a completely different string altogether. For example –

```
#!/usr/bin/python


var1 = 'Hello World!'

print "Updated String :- ", var1[:6] + 'Python'
```

When the above code is executed, it produces the following result –

```
Updated String :-  Hello Python
```

Escape Characters

Following table is a list of escape or non-printable characters that can be represented with backslash notation.

An escape character gets interpreted; in a single quoted as well as double quoted strings.

Backslash notation	Hexadecimal character	Description
\a	0x07	Bell or alert
\b	0x08	Backspace
\cx		Control-x

\C-x		Control-x
\e	0x1b	Escape
\f	0x0c	Formfeed
\M-\C-x		Meta-Control-x
\n	0x0a	Newline
\nnn		Octal notation, where n is in the range 0.7
\r	0x0d	Carriage return
\s	0x20	Space
\t	0x09	Tab
\v	0x0b	Vertical tab

\x	Character x
\xnn	Hexadecimal notation, where n is in the range 0.9, a.f, or A.F

String Special Operators

Assume string variable a holds 'Hello' and variable b holds 'Python', then −

Operator	Description	Example
+	Concatenation - Adds values on either side of the operator	a + b will give HelloPython
*	Repetition - Creates new strings, concatenating multiple copies of the same string	a*2 will give -HelloHello
[]	Slice - Gives the character from the given index	a[1] will give e

[:]	Range Slice - Gives the characters from the given range	a[1:4] will give ell
in	Membership - Returns true if a character exists in the given string	H in a will give 1
not in	Membership - Returns true if a character does not exist in the given string	M not in a will give 1
r/R	Raw String - Suppresses actual meaning of Escape characters. The syntax for raw strings is exactly the same as for normal strings with the exception of the raw string operator, the letter "r," which precedes the quotation marks. The "r" can be lowercase (r) or uppercase (R) and must be placed immediately preceding the first quote mark.	print r'\n' prints \n and print R'\n'prints \n
%	Format - Performs String formatting	See at next section

String Formatting Operator

One of Python's coolest features is the string format operator %. This operator is unique to strings and makes up for the pack of having functions from C's printf() family. Following is a simple example –

```
#!/usr/bin/python

print "My name is %s and weight is %d kg!" % ('Zara', 21)
```

When the above code is executed, it produces the following result –

```
My name is Zara and weight is 21 kg!
```

Here is the list of complete set of symbols which can be used along with % –

Format Symbol	Conversion
%c	Character
%s	string conversion via str() prior to formatting
%i	signed decimal integer

%d	signed decimal integer
%u	unsigned decimal integer
%o	octal integer
%x	hexadecimal integer (lowercase letters)
%X	hexadecimal integer (UPPERcase letters)
%e	exponential notation (with lowercase 'e')
%E	exponential notation (with UPPERcase 'E')
%f	floating point real number
%g	the shorter of %f and %e

Symbol	Functionality
%G	the shorter of %f and %E

Other supported symbols and functionality are listed in the following table –

Symbol	Functionality
*	argument specifies width or precision
-	left justification
+	display the sign
<sp>	leave a blank space before a positive number
#	add the octal leading zero ('0') or hexadecimal leading '0x' or '0X', depending on whether 'x' or 'X' were used.
0	pad from left with zeros (instead of spaces)
%	'%%' leaves you with a single literal '%'

(var)	mapping variable (dictionary arguments)
m.n.	m is the minimum total width and n is the number of digits to display after the decimal point (if appl.)

Triple Quotes

Python's triple quotes comes to the rescue by allowing strings to span multiple lines, including verbatim NEWLINEs, TABs, and any other special characters.

The syntax for triple quotes consists of three consecutive single or doublequotes.

```
#!/usr/bin/python

para_str = """this is a long string that is made up of

several lines and non-printable characters such as

TAB ( \t ) and they will show up that way when displayed.

NEWLINEs within the string, whether explicitly given like

this within the brackets [ \n ], or just a NEWLINE within

the variable assignment will also show up.
"""

print para_str
```

When the above code is executed, it produces the following result. Note how every single special character has been converted to its printed form, right down to the last NEWLINE at the end of the string between the "up." and closing triple quotes. Also note that NEWLINEs occur either with an explicit carriage return at the end of a line or its escape code (\n) –

this is a long string that is made up of

several lines and non-printable characters such as

TAB (   ) and they will show up that way when displayed.

NEWLINEs within the string, whether explicitly given like

this within the brackets [

], or just a NEWLINE within

the variable assignment will also show up.

Raw strings do not treat the backslash as a special character at all. Every character you put into a raw string stays the way you wrote it –

```
#!/usr/bin/python
```

```
print 'C:\\nowhere'
```

When the above code is executed, it produces the following result –

C:\nowhere

Now let's make use of raw string. We would put expression in r'expression'as follows –

```
#!/usr/bin/python
```

```
print r'C:\\nowhere'
```

When the above code is executed, it produces the following result –

```
C:\\nowhere
```

Unicode String

Normal strings in Python are stored internally as 8-bit ASCII, while Unicode strings are stored as 16-bit Unicode. This allows for a more varied set of characters, including special characters from most languages in the world. I'll restrict my treatment of Unicode strings to the following –

```
#!/usr/bin/python


print u'Hello, world!'
```

When the above code is executed, it produces the following result –

```
Hello, world!
```

As you can see, Unicode strings use the prefix u, just as raw strings use the prefix r.

METHODS

Built-in String Methods

Python includes the following built-in methods to manipulate strings –

Sr.No.	Methods with Description
1	**capitalize()** Capitalizes first letter of string
2	**center(width, fillchar)** Returns a space-padded string with the original string centered to a total of width columns.
3	**count(str, beg= 0,end=len(string))** Counts how many times str occurs in string or in a substring of string if starting index beg and ending index end are given.
4	**decode(encoding='UTF-8',errors='strict')** Decodes the string using the codec registered for encoding. encoding defaults to the default string encoding.
5	**encode(encoding='UTF-8',errors='strict')**

Returns encoded string version of string; on error, default is to raise a ValueError unless errors is given with 'ignore' or 'replace'.

6   **endswith(suffix, beg=0, end=len(string))**

Determines if string or a substring of string (if starting index beg and ending index end are given) ends with suffix; returns true if so and false otherwise.

7   **expandtabs(tabsize=8)**

Expands tabs in string to multiple spaces; defaults to 8 spaces per tab if tabsize not provided.

8   **find(str, beg=0 end=len(string))**

Determine if str occurs in string or in a substring of string if starting index beg and ending index end are given returns index if found and -1 otherwise.

9   **index(str, beg=0, end=len(string))**

Same as find(), but raises an exception if str not found.

10   **isalnum()**

Returns true if string has at least 1 character and all characters are alphanumeric and false otherwise.

11	**isalpha()**
	Returns true if string has at least 1 character and all characters are alphabetic and false otherwise.

12	**isdigit()**
	Returns true if string contains only digits and false otherwise.

13	**islower()**
	Returns true if string has at least 1 cased character and all cased characters are in lowercase and false otherwise.

14	**isnumeric()**
	Returns true if a unicode string contains only numeric characters and false otherwise.

15	**isspace()**
	Returns true if string contains only whitespace characters and false otherwise.

16	**istitle()**
	Returns true if string is properly "titlecased" and false otherwise.

17	**isupper()**

Returns true if string has at least one cased character and all cased characters are in uppercase and false otherwise.

18   **join(seq)**

Merges (concatenates) the string representations of elements in sequence seq into a string, with separator string.

19   **len(string)**

Returns the length of the string

20   **ljust(width[, fillchar])**

Returns a space-padded string with the original string left-justified to a total of width columns.

21   **lower()**

Converts all uppercase letters in string to lowercase.

22   **lstrip()**

Removes all leading whitespace in string.

23   **maketrans()**

Returns a translation table to be used in translate function.

24	**max(str)**
	Returns the max alphabetical character from the string str.

25	**min(str)**
	Returns the min alphabetical character from the string str.

26	**replace(old, new [, max])**
	Replaces all occurrences of old in string with new or at most max occurrences if max given.

27	**rfind(str, beg=0,end=len(string))**
	Same as find(), but search backwards in string.

28	**rindex(str, beg=0, end=len(string))**
	Same as index(), but search backwards in string.

29	**rjust(width,[, fillchar])**
	Returns a space-padded string with the original string right-justified to a total of width columns.

30	**rstrip()**
	Removes all trailing whitespace of string.

31	**split(str="", num=string.count(str))**

Splits string according to delimiter str (space if not provided) and returns list of substrings; split into at most num substrings if given.

32   **splitlines(num=string.count('\n'))**

Splits string at all (or num) NEWLINEs and returns a list of each line with NEWLINEs removed.

33   **startswith(str, beg=0,end=len(string))**

Determines if string or a substring of string (if starting index beg and ending index end are given) starts with substring str; returns true if so and false otherwise.

34   **strip([chars])**

Performs both lstrip() and rstrip() on string.

35   **swapcase()**

Inverts case for all letters in string.

36   **title()**

Returns "titlecased" version of string, that is, all words begin with uppercase and the rest are lowercase.

37   **translate(table, deletechars="")**

Translates string according to translation table str(256 chars), removing those in the del string.

38	**upper()**
	Converts lowercase letters in string to uppercase.

39	**zfill (width)**
	Returns original string leftpadded with zeros to a total of width characters; intended for numbers, zfill() retains any sign given (less one zero).

40	**isdecimal()**
	Returns true if a unicode string contains only decimal characters and false otherwise.

The most basic data structure in Python is the sequence. Each element of a sequence is assigned a number - its position or index. The first index is zero, the second index is one, and so forth.

Python has six built-in types of sequences, but the most common ones are lists and tuples, which we would see in this tutorial.

There are certain things you can do with all sequence types. These operations include indexing, slicing, adding, multiplying, and checking for membership. In addition, Python has built-in functions for finding the length of a sequence and for finding its largest and smallest elements.

PYTHON LISTS

The list is a most versatile datatype available in Python which can be written as a list of comma-separated values (items) between square brackets. Important thing about a list is that items in a list need not be of the same type.

Creating a list is as simple as putting different comma-separated values between square brackets. For example –

```
list1 = ['physics', 'chemistry', 1997, 2000];

list2 = [1, 2, 3, 4, 5 ];

list3 = ["a", "b", "c", "d"]
```

Similar to string indices, list indices start at 0, and lists can be sliced, concatenated and so on.

Accessing Values in Lists

To access values in lists, use the square brackets for slicing along with the index or indices to obtain value available at that index. For example –

```
#!/usr/bin/python


list1 = ['physics', 'chemistry', 1997, 2000];

list2 = [1, 2, 3, 4, 5, 6, 7 ];

print "list1[0]: ", list1[0]

print "list2[1:5]: ", list2[1:5]
```

When the above code is executed, it produces the following result –

```
list1[0]:  physics
list2[1:5]:  [2, 3, 4, 5]
```

Updating Lists

You can update single or multiple elements of lists by giving the slice on the left-hand side of the assignment operator, and you can add to elements in a list with the append() method. For example –

```
#!/usr/bin/python


list = ['physics', 'chemistry', 1997, 2000];

print "Value available at index 2 : "

print list[2]

list[2] = 2001;

print "New value available at index 2 : "

print list[2]
```

Note – append() method is discussed in subsequent section.

When the above code is executed, it produces the following result –

```
Value available at index 2 :
1997
```

New value available at index 2 :

2001

Delete List Elements

To remove a list element, you can use either the del statement if you know exactly which element(s) you are deleting or the remove() method if you do not know. For example –

```
#!/usr/bin/python


list1 = ['physics', 'chemistry', 1997, 2000];

print list1

del list1[2];

print "After deleting value at index 2 : "

print list1
```

When the above code is executed, it produces following result –

```
['physics', 'chemistry', 1997, 2000]
After deleting value at index 2 :
['physics', 'chemistry', 2000]
```

Note – remove() method is discussed in subsequent section.

Basic List Operations

Lists respond to the + and * operators much like strings; they mean concatenation and repetition here too, except that the result is a new list, not a string.

In fact, lists respond to all of the general sequence operations we used on strings in the prior chapter.

Python Expression	Results	Description
len([1, 2, 3])	3	Length
[1, 2, 3] + [4, 5, 6]	[1, 2, 3, 4, 5, 6]	Concatenation
['Hi!'] * 4	['Hi!', 'Hi!', 'Hi!', 'Hi!']	Repetition
3 in [1, 2, 3]	True	Membership
for x in [1, 2, 3]: print x,	1 2 3	Iteration

Indexing, Slicing, and Matrixes

Because lists are sequences, indexing and slicing work the same way for lists as they do for strings.

Assuming following input –

L = ['spam', 'Spam', 'SPAM!']

Python Expression	Results	Description
L[2]	SPAM!	Offsets start at zero
L[-2]	Spam	Negative: count from the right
L[1:]	['Spam', 'SPAM!']	Slicing fetches sections

Built-in List Functions & Methods

Python includes the following list functions –

Sr.No.	Function with Description
1	**cmp(list1, list2)** Compares elements of both lists.
2	**len(list)** Gives the total length of the list.
3	**max(list)** Returns item from the list with max value.
4	**min(list)** Returns item from the list with min value.
5	**list(seq)** Converts a tuple into list.

Python includes following list methods

Sr.No.	Methods with Description
1	**list.append(obj)** Appends object obj to list
2	**list.count(obj)** Returns count of how many times obj occurs in list
3	**list.extend(seq)** Appends the contents of seq to list
4	**list.index(obj)** Returns the lowest index in list that obj appears
5	**list.insert(index, obj)** Inserts object obj into list at offset index
6	**list.pop(obj=list[-1])** Removes and returns last object or obj from list

| 7 | **list.remove(obj)** |
| | Removes object obj from list |

| 8 | **list.reverse()** |
| | Reverses objects of list in place |

| 9 | **list.sort([func])** |
| | Sorts objects of list, use compare func if given |

TUPLE

A tuple is a sequence of immutable Python objects. Tuples are sequences, just like lists. The differences between tuples and lists are, the tuples cannot be changed unlike lists and tuples use parentheses, whereas lists use square brackets.

Creating a tuple is as simple as putting different comma-separated values. Optionally you can put these comma-separated values between parentheses also. For example –

```
tup1 = ('physics', 'chemistry', 1997, 2000);

tup2 = (1, 2, 3, 4, 5 );

tup3 = "a", "b", "c", "d";
```

The empty tuple is written as two parentheses containing nothing –

```
tup1 = ();
```

To write a tuple containing a single value you have to include a comma, even though there is only one value –

```
tup1 = (50,);
```

Like string indices, tuple indices start at 0, and they can be sliced, concatenated, and so on.

Accessing Values in Tuples

To access values in tuple, use the square brackets for slicing along with the index or indices to obtain value available at that index. For example –

```
#!/usr/bin/python


tup1 = ('physics', 'chemistry', 1997, 2000);

tup2 = (1, 2, 3, 4, 5, 6, 7 );

print "tup1[0]: ", tup1[0];

print "tup2[1:5]: ", tup2[1:5];
```

When the above code is executed, it produces the following result –

```
tup1[0]:  physics
tup2[1:5]:  [2, 3, 4, 5]
```

Updating Tuples

Tuples are immutable which means you cannot update or change the values of tuple elements. You are able to take portions of existing tuples to create new tuples as the following example demonstrates –

```
#!/usr/bin/python


tup1 = (12, 34.56);

tup2 = ('abc', 'xyz');


# Following action is not valid for tuples

# tup1[0] = 100;
```

```
# So let's create a new tuple as follows

tup3 = tup1 + tup2;

print tup3;
```

When the above code is executed, it produces the following result –

```
(12, 34.56, 'abc', 'xyz')
```

Delete Tuple Elements

Removing individual tuple elements is not possible. There is, of course, nothing wrong with putting together another tuple with the undesired elements discarded.

To explicitly remove an entire tuple, just use the del statement. For example –

```
#!/usr/bin/python


tup = ('physics', 'chemistry', 1997, 2000);

print tup;

del tup;

print "After deleting tup : ";

print tup;
```

This produces the following result. Note an exception raised, this is because after del tup tuple does not exist any more –

('physics', 'chemistry', 1997, 2000)

After deleting tup :

Traceback (most recent call last):

  File "test.py", line 9, in <module>

    print tup;

NameError: name 'tup' is not defined

Basic Tuples Operations

Tuples respond to the + and * operators much like strings; they mean concatenation and repetition here too, except that the result is a new tuple, not a string.

In fact, tuples respond to all of the general sequence operations we used on strings in the prior chapter –

Python Expression	Results	Description
len((1, 2, 3))	3	Length
(1, 2, 3) + (4, 5, 6)	(1, 2, 3, 4, 5, 6)	Concatenation
('Hi!',) * 4	('Hi!', 'Hi!', 'Hi!', 'Hi!')	Repetition

3 in (1, 2, 3)	True	Membership
for x in (1, 2, 3): print x,	1 2 3	Iteration

Indexing, Slicing, and Matrixes

Because tuples are sequences, indexing and slicing work the same way for tuples as they do for strings. Assuming following input –

```
L = ('spam', 'Spam', 'SPAM!')
```

Python Expression	Results	Description
L[2]	'SPAM!'	Offsets start at zero
L[-2]	'Spam'	Negative: count from the right
L[1:]	['Spam', 'SPAM!']	Slicing fetches sections

No Enclosing Delimiters

Any set of multiple objects, comma-separated, written without identifying symbols, i.e., brackets for lists, parentheses for tuples, etc., default to tuples, as indicated in these short examples –

```
#!/usr/bin/python


print 'abc', -4.24e93, 18+6.6j, 'xyz';

x, y = 1, 2;

print "Value of x , y : ", x,y;
```

When the above code is executed, it produces the following result –

```
abc -4.24e+93 (18+6.6j) xyz
Value of x , y : 1 2
```

Built-in Tuple Functions

Python includes the following tuple functions –

Sr.No.	Function with Description
1	**cmp(tuple1, tuple2)** Compares elements of both tuples.

2	**len(tuple)**

Gives the total length of the tuple.

3	**max(tuple)**

Returns item from the tuple with max value.

4	**min(tuple)**

Returns item from the tuple with min value.

5	**tuple(seq)**

Converts a list into tuple.

Each key is separated from its value by a colon (:), the items are separated by commas, and the whole thing is enclosed in curly braces. An empty dictionary without any items is written with just two curly braces, like this: {}.

Keys are unique within a dictionary while values may not be. The values of a dictionary can be of any type, but the keys must be of an immutable data type such as strings, numbers, or tuples.

DIRECTORIES

To access dictionary elements, you can use the familiar square brackets along with the key to obtain its value. Following is a simple example –

```
#!/usr/bin/python


dict = {'Name': 'Zara', 'Age': 7, 'Class': 'First'}

print "dict['Name']: ", dict['Name']

print "dict['Age']: ", dict['Age']
```

When the above code is executed, it produces the following result –

```
dict['Name']:  Zara
dict['Age']:  7
```

If we attempt to access a data item with a key, which is not part of the dictionary, we get an error as follows –

```
#!/usr/bin/python


dict = {'Name': 'Zara', 'Age': 7, 'Class': 'First'}

print "dict['Alice']: ", dict['Alice']
```

When the above code is executed, it produces the following result –

```
dict['Alice']:
```

```
Traceback (most recent call last):
    File "test.py", line 4, in <module>
        print "dict['Alice']: ", dict['Alice'];
KeyError: 'Alice'
```

Updating Dictionary

You can update a dictionary by adding a new entry or a key-value pair, modifying an existing entry, or deleting an existing entry as shown below in the simple example –

```
#!/usr/bin/python

dict = {'Name': 'Zara', 'Age': 7, 'Class': 'First'}

dict['Age'] = 8; # update existing entry

dict['School'] = "DPS School"; # Add new entry


print "dict['Age']: ", dict['Age']

print "dict['School']: ", dict['School']
```

When the above code is executed, it produces the following result –

```
dict['Age']:  8
dict['School']:  DPS School
```

Delete Dictionary Elements

You can either remove individual dictionary elements or clear the entire contents of a dictionary. You can also delete entire dictionary in a single operation.

To explicitly remove an entire dictionary, just use the del statement. Following is a simple example –

```
#!/usr/bin/python


dict = {'Name': 'Zara', 'Age': 7, 'Class': 'First'}

del dict['Name']; # remove entry with key 'Name'

dict.clear();      # remove all entries in dict

del dict ;         # delete entire dictionary


print "dict['Age']: ", dict['Age']

print "dict['School']: ", dict['School']
```

This produces the following result. Note that an exception is raised because after del dict dictionary does not exist any more –

```
Traceback (most recent call last):
   File "test.py", line 8, in <module>
     print "dict['Age']: ", dict['Age'];
```

TypeError: 'type' object is unsubscriptable

Note – del() method is discussed in subsequent section.

Properties of Dictionary Keys

Dictionary values have no restrictions. They can be any arbitrary Python object, either standard objects or user-defined objects. However, same is not true for the keys.

There are two important points to remember about dictionary keys –

(a) More than one entry per key not allowed. Which means no duplicate key is allowed. When duplicate keys encountered during assignment, the last assignment wins. For example –

```
#!/usr/bin/python


dict = {'Name': 'Zara', 'Age': 7, 'Name': 'Manni'}

print "dict['Name']: ", dict['Name']
```

When the above code is executed, it produces the following result –

```
dict['Name']:  Manni
```

(b) Keys must be immutable. Which means you can use strings, numbers or tuples as dictionary keys but something like ['key'] is not allowed. Following is a simple example –

```
#!/usr/bin/python

dict = {['Name']: 'Zara', 'Age': 7}

print "dict['Name']: ", dict['Name']
```

When the above code is executed, it produces the following result –

```
Traceback (most recent call last):
  File "test.py", line 3, in <module>
    dict = {['Name']: 'Zara', 'Age': 7};
TypeError: unhashable type: 'list'
```

Built-in Dictionary Functions & Methods

Python includes the following dictionary functions –

Sr.No.	Function with Description
1	**cmp(dict1, dict2)** Compares elements of both dict.
2	**len(dict)** Gives the total length of the dictionary. This would be equal to the number of items in the dictionary.
3	**str(dict)** Produces a printable string representation of a dictionary
4	**type(variable)**

Returns the type of the passed variable. If passed variable is dictionary, then it would return a dictionary type.

Python includes following dictionary methods –

Sr.No.	Methods with Description
1	**dict.clear()** Removes all elements of dictionary *dict*
2	**dict.copy()** Returns a shallow copy of dictionary *dict*
3	**dict.fromkeys()** Create a new dictionary with keys from seq and values *set* to *value*.
4	**dict.get(key, default=None)** For *key* key, returns value or default if key not in dictionary
5	**dict.has_key(key)** Returns *true* if key in dictionary *dict*, *false* otherwise

6	**dict.items()**
	Returns a list of *dict*'s (key, value) tuple pairs

7	**dict.keys()**
	Returns list of dictionary dict's keys

8	**dict.setdefault(key, default=None)**
	Similar to get(), but will set dict[key]=default if *key* is not already in dict

9	**dict.update(dict2)**
	Adds dictionary *dict2*'s key-values pairs to *dict*

10	**dict.values()**
	Returns list of dictionary *dict*'s values

A Python program can handle date and time in several ways. Converting between date formats is a common chore for computers. Python's time and calendar modules help track dates and times.

TIME

Time intervals are floating-point numbers in units of seconds. Particular instants in time are expressed in seconds since 12:00am, January 1, 1970(epoch).

There is a popular time module available in Python which provides functions for working with times, and for converting between representations. The function time.time() returns the current system time in ticks since 12:00am, January 1, 1970(epoch).

Example

```
#!/usr/bin/python

import time;  # This is required to include time module.

ticks = time.time()

print "Number of ticks since 12:00am, January 1, 1970:", ticks
```

This would produce a result something as follows −

```
Number of ticks since 12:00am, January 1, 1970:
7186862.73399
```

Date arithmetic is easy to do with ticks. However, dates before the epoch cannot be represented in this form. Dates in the far future also cannot be represented this way - the cutoff point is sometime in 2038 for UNIX and Windows.

What is TimeTuple?

Many of Python's time functions handle time as a tuple of 9 numbers, as shown below –

Index	Field	Values
0	4-digit year	2008
1	Month	1 to 12
2	Day	1 to 31
3	Hour	0 to 23
4	Minute	0 to 59
5	Second	0 to 61 (60 or 61 are leap-seconds)
6	Day of Week	0 to 6 (0 is Monday)
7	Day of year	1 to 366 (Julian day)

| 8 | Daylight savings | -1, 0, 1, -1 means library determines DST |

The above tuple is equivalent to struct_time structure. This structure has following attributes –

Index	Attributes	Values
0	tm_year	2008
1	tm_mon	1 to 12
2	tm_mday	1 to 31
3	tm_hour	0 to 23
4	tm_min	0 to 59
5	tm_sec	0 to 61 (60 or 61 are leap-seconds)
6	tm_wday	0 to 6 (0 is Monday)

| 7 | tm_yday | 1 to 366 (Julian day) |
| 8 | tm_isdst | -1, 0, 1, -1 means library determines DST |

Getting current time

To translate a time instant from a seconds since the epoch floating-point value into a time-tuple, pass the floating-point value to a function (e.g., localtime) that returns a time-tuple with all nine items valid.

```
#!/usr/bin/python

import time;


localtime = time.localtime(time.time())

print "Local current time :", localtime
```

This would produce the following result, which could be formatted in any other presentable form –

```
Local current time : time.struct_time(tm_year=2013, tm_mon=7,

tm_mday=17, tm_hour=21, tm_min=26, tm_sec=3, tm_wday=2, tm_yday=198, tm_isdst=0)
```

Getting formatted time

You can format any time as per your requirement, but simple method to get time in readable format is asctime() –

```
#!/usr/bin/python

import time;


localtime = time.asctime( time.localtime(time.time()) )

print "Local current time :", localtime
```

This would produce the following result –

```
Local current time : Tue Jan 13 10:17:09 2009
```

Getting calendar for a month

The calendar module gives a wide range of methods to play with yearly and monthly calendars. Here, we print a calendar for a given month (Jan 2008) –

```
#!/usr/bin/python

import calendar

cal = calendar.month(2008, 1)

print "Here is the calendar:"

print cal
```

This would produce the following result –

Here is the calendar:

Here is the calendar:

```
   January 2008
Mo Tu We Th Fr Sa Su
    1  2  3  4  5  6
 7  8  9 10 11 12 13
14 15 16 17 18 19 20
21 22 23 24 25 26 27
28 29 30 31
```

The time Module

There is a popular time module available in Python which provides functions for working with times and for converting between representations. Here is the list of all available methods –

Sr.No.	Function with Description
1	**time.altzone** The offset of the local DST timezone, in seconds west of UTC, if one is defined. This is negative if the local DST timezone is east of UTC (as in Western Europe, including the UK). Only use this if daylight is nonzero.

2   **time.asctime([tupletime])**

Accepts a time-tuple and returns a readable 24-character string such as 'Tue Dec 11 18:07:14 2008'.

3   **time.clock( )**

Returns the current CPU time as a floating-point number of seconds. To measure computational costs of different approaches, the value of time.clock is more useful than that of time.time().

4   **time.ctime([secs])**

Like   asctime(localtime(secs))   and   without arguments is like asctime( )

5   **time.gmtime([secs])**

Accepts an instant expressed in seconds since the epoch and returns a time-tuple t with the UTC time. Note : t.tm_isdst is always 0

6   **time.localtime([secs])**

Accepts an instant expressed in seconds since the epoch and returns a time-tuple t with the local time (t.tm_isdst is 0 or 1, depending on whether DST applies to instant secs by local rules).

7 **time.mktime(tupletime)**

Accepts an instant expressed as a time-tuple in local time and returns a floating-point value with the instant expressed in seconds since the epoch.

8 **time.sleep(secs)**

Suspends the calling thread for secs seconds.

9 **time.strftime(fmt[,tupletime])**

Accepts an instant expressed as a time-tuple in local time and returns a string representing the instant as specified by string fmt.

10 **time.strptime(str,fmt='%a %b %d %H:%M:%S %Y')**

Parses str according to format string fmt and returns the instant in time-tuple format.

11 **time.time( )**

Returns the current time instant, a floating-point number of seconds since the epoch.

12	**time.tzset()**

> Resets the time conversion rules used by the library routines. The environment variable TZ specifies how this is done.

Resets the time conversion rules used by the library routines. The environment variable TZ specifies how this is done.

Let us go through the functions briefly –

There are following two important attributes available with time module –

Sr.No.	Attribute with Description
1	**time.timezone** Attribute time.timezone is the offset in seconds of the local time zone (without DST) from UTC (>0 in the Americas; <=0 in most of Europe, Asia, Africa).
2	**time.tzname** Attribute time.tzname is a pair of locale-dependent strings, which are the names of the local time zone without and with DST, respectively.

The calendar Module

The calendar module supplies calendar-related functions, including functions to print a text calendar for a given month or year.

By default, calendar takes Monday as the first day of the week and Sunday as the last one. To change this, call calendar.setfirstweekday() function.

Here is a list of functions available with the calendar module –

Sr.No.	Function with Description
1	**calendar.calendar(year,w=2,l=1,c=6)** Returns a multiline string with a calendar for year year formatted into three columns separated by c spaces. w is the width in characters of each date; each line has length $21*w+18+2*c$. l is the number of lines for each week.
2	**calendar.firstweekday( )** Returns the current setting for the weekday that starts each week. By default, when calendar is first imported, this is 0, meaning Monday.
3	**calendar.isleap(year)** Returns True if year is a leap year; otherwise, False.

4   **calendar.leapdays(y1,y2)**

Returns the total number of leap days in the years within range(y1,y2).

5   **calendar.month(year,month,w=2,l=1)**

Returns a multiline string with a calendar for month month of year year, one line per week plus two header lines. w is the width in characters of each date; each line has length 7*w+6. l is the number of lines for each week.

6   **calendar.monthcalendar(year,month)**

Returns a list of lists of ints. Each sublist denotes a week. Days outside month month of year year are set to 0; days within the month are set to their day-of-month, 1 and up.

7   **calendar.monthrange(year,month)**

Returns two integers. The first one is the code of the weekday for the first day of the month month in year year; the second one is the number of days in the month. Weekday codes are 0 (Monday) to 6 (Sunday); month numbers are 1 to 12.

8   **calendar.prcal(year,w=2,l=1,c=6)**

Like print calendar.calendar(year,w,l,c).

9   **calendar.prmonth(year,month,w=2,l=1)**

Like print calendar.month(year,month,w,l).

10   **calendar.setfirstweekday(weekday)**

Sets the first day of each week to weekday code
weekday. Weekday codes are 0 (Monday) to 6
(Sunday).

11   **calendar.timegm(tupletime)**

The inverse of time.gmtime: accepts a time
instant in time-tuple form and returns the same
instant as a floating-point number of seconds
since the epoch.

12   **calendar.weekday(year,month,day)**

Returns the weekday code for the given date.
Weekday codes are 0 (Monday) to 6 (Sunday);
month numbers are 1 (January) to 12
(December).

MODULES & FUNCTIONS

If you are interested, then here you would find a list of other important modules and functions to play with date & time in Python –

- The datetime Module

- The pytz Module

- The dateutil Module

A function is a block of organized, reusable code that is used to perform a single, related action. Functions provide better modularity for your application and a high degree of code reusing.

As you already know, Python gives you many built-in functions like print(), etc. but you can also create your own functions. These functions are called user-defined functions.

Defining a Function

You can define functions to provide the required functionality. Here are simple rules to define a function in Python.

- Function blocks begin with the keyword def followed by the function name and parentheses (( )).

- Any input parameters or arguments should be placed within these parentheses. You can also define parameters inside these parentheses.

- The first statement of a function can be an optional statement - the documentation string of the function or docstring.

- The code block within every function starts with a colon (:) and is indented.

- The statement return [expression] exits a function, optionally passing back an expression to the caller. A return statement with no arguments is the same as return None.

Syntax

```
def functionname( parameters ):

    "function_docstring"

    function_suite

    return [expression]
```

By default, parameters have a positional behavior and you need to inform them in the same order that they were defined.

Example

The following function takes a string as input parameter and prints it on standard screen.

```
def printme( str ):

    "This prints a passed string into this function"

    print str

    return
```

Calling a Function

Defining a function only gives it a name, specifies the parameters that are to be included in the function and structures the blocks of code.

Once the basic structure of a function is finalized, you can execute it by calling it from another function or directly from the Python prompt. Following is the example to call printme() function –

```
#!/usr/bin/python


# Function definition is here

def printme( str ):

    "This prints a passed string into this function"

    print str

    return;


# Now you can call printme function

printme("I'm first call to user defined function!")

printme("Again second call to the same function")
```

When the above code is executed, it produces the following result –

```
I'm first call to user defined function!

Again second call to the same function
```

Pass by reference vs value

All parameters (arguments) in the Python language are passed by reference. It means if you change what a parameter refers to within a function, the change also reflects back in the calling function. For example –

```
#!/usr/bin/python


# Function definition is here

def changeme( mylist ):

   "This changes a passed list into this function"

   mylist.append([1,2,3,4]);

   print "Values inside the function: ", mylist

   return


# Now you can call changeme function

mylist = [10,20,30];

changeme( mylist );

print "Values outside the function: ", mylist
```

Here, we are maintaining reference of the passed object and appending values in the same object. So, this would produce the following result –

```
Values inside the function:  [10, 20, 30, [1, 2, 3, 4]]

Values outside the function:  [10, 20, 30, [1, 2, 3, 4]]
```

There is one more example where argument is being passed by reference and the reference is being overwritten inside the called function.

```
#!/usr/bin/python


# Function definition is here

def changeme( mylist ):

    "This changes a passed list into this function"

    mylist = [1,2,3,4]; # This would assig new reference in mylist

    print "Values inside the function: ", mylist


    return


# Now you can call changeme function

mylist = [10,20,30];

changeme( mylist );

print "Values outside the function: ", mylist
```

The parameter mylist is local to the function changeme. Changing mylist within the function does not affect mylist. The function accomplishes nothing and finally this would produce the following result –

Values inside the function: [1, 2, 3, 4]

Values outside the function: [10, 20, 30]

Function Arguments

You can call a function by using the following types of formal arguments −

- Required arguments
- Keyword arguments
- Default arguments
- Variable-length arguments

Required arguments

Required arguments are the arguments passed to a function in correct positional order. Here, the number of arguments in the function call should match exactly with the function definition.

To call the function printme(), you definitely need to pass one argument, otherwise it gives a syntax error as follows −

```
#!/usr/bin/python


# Function definition is here

def printme( str ):

   "This prints a passed string into this function"

   print str
```

```
    return;
```

```
# Now you can call printme function
```

```
printme()
```

When the above code is executed, it produces the following result –

```
Traceback (most recent call last):
    File "test.py", line 11, in <module>
        printme();
TypeError: printme() takes exactly 1 argument (0 given)
```

Keyword arguments

Keyword arguments are related to the function calls. When you use keyword arguments in a function call, the caller identifies the arguments by the parameter name.

This allows you to skip arguments or place them out of order because the Python interpreter is able to use the keywords provided to match the values with parameters. You can also make keyword calls to the printme() function in the following ways –

```
#!/usr/bin/python
```

```
# Function definition is here
```

```
def printme( str ):
```

```
    "This prints a passed string into this function"

    print str

    return;


# Now you can call printme function
printme( str = "My string")
```

When the above code is executed, it produces the following result –

```
My string
```

The following example gives more clear picture. Note that the order of parameters does not matter.

```
#!/usr/bin/python


# Function definition is here
def printinfo( name, age ):

    "This prints a passed info into this function"

    print "Name: ", name

    print "Age ", age

    return;


# Now you can call printinfo function
```

```
printinfo( age=50, name="miki" )
```

When the above code is executed, it produces the following result –

```
Name:  miki

Age  50
```

Default arguments

A default argument is an argument that assumes a default value if a value is not provided in the function call for that argument. The following example gives an idea on default arguments, it prints default age if it is not passed –

```
#!/usr/bin/python


# Function definition is here

def printinfo( name, age = 35 ):

   "This prints a passed info into this function"

   print "Name: ", name

   print "Age ", age

   return;


# Now you can call printinfo function

printinfo( age=50, name="miki" )
```

```
printinfo( name="miki" )
```

When the above code is executed, it produces the following result –

```
Name: miki
Age 50
Name: miki
Age 35
```

Variable-length arguments

You may need to process a function for more arguments than you specified while defining the function. These arguments are called variable-lengtharguments and are not named in the function definition, unlike required and default arguments.

Syntax for a function with non-keyword variable arguments is this –

```
def functionname([formal_args,] *var_args_tuple ):
   "function_docstring"
   function_suite
   return [expression]
```

An asterisk (*) is placed before the variable name that holds the values of all nonkeyword variable arguments. This tuple remains empty if no additional arguments are specified during the function call. Following is a simple example –

```
#!/usr/bin/python
```

```
# Function definition is here

def printinfo( arg1, *vartuple ):

    "This prints a variable passed arguments"

    print "Output is: "

    print arg1

    for var in vartuple:

        print var

    return;


# Now you can call printinfo function

printinfo( 10 )

printinfo( 70, 60, 50 )
```

When the above code is executed, it produces the following result –

```
Output is:

10

Output is:

70

60

50
```

The Anonymous Functions

These functions are called anonymous because they are not declared in the standard manner by using the def keyword. You can use the lambda keyword to create small anonymous functions.

- Lambda forms can take any number of arguments but return just one value in the form of an expression. They cannot contain commands or multiple expressions.

- An anonymous function cannot be a direct call to print because lambda requires an expression

- Lambda functions have their own local namespace and cannot access variables other than those in their parameter list and those in the global namespace.

- Although it appears that lambda's are a one-line version of a function, they are not equivalent to inline statements in C or C++, whose purpose is by passing function stack allocation during invocation for performance reasons.

SYNTAX

The syntax of lambda functions contains only a single statement, which is as follows –

```
lambda [arg1 [,arg2,.....argn]]:expression
```

Following is the example to show how lambda form of function works –

```
#!/usr/bin/python


# Function definition is here
```

```
sum = lambda arg1, arg2: arg1 + arg2;


# Now you can call sum as a function

print "Value of total : ", sum( 10, 20 )

print "Value of total : ", sum( 20, 20 )
```

When the above code is executed, it produces the following result –

```
Value of total :  30

Value of total :  40
```

The return Statement

The statement return [expression] exits a function, optionally passing back an expression to the caller. A return statement with no arguments is the same as return None.

All the above examples are not returning any value. You can return a value from a function as follows –

```
#!/usr/bin/python


# Function definition is here

def sum( arg1, arg2 ):

    # Add both the parameters and return them."
```

```
   total = arg1 + arg2

   print "Inside the function : ", total

   return total;


# Now you can call sum function

total = sum( 10, 20 );

print "Outside the function : ", total
```

When the above code is executed, it produces the following result –

```
Inside the function :  30
Outside the function :  30
```

Scope of Variables

All variables in a program may not be accessible at all locations in that program. This depends on where you have declared a variable.

The scope of a variable determines the portion of the program where you can access a particular identifier. There are two basic scopes of variables in Python –

- Global variables
- Local variables

Global vs. Local variables

Variables that are defined inside a function body have a local scope, and those defined outside have a global scope.

This means that local variables can be accessed only inside the function in which they are declared, whereas global variables can be accessed throughout the program body by all functions. When you call a function, the variables declared inside it are brought into scope. Following is a simple example –

```
#!/usr/bin/python


total = 0; # This is global variable.

# Function definition is here

def sum( arg1, arg2 ):

    # Add both the parameters and return them."

    total = arg1 + arg2; # Here total is local variable.

    print "Inside the function local total : ", total

    return total;


# Now you can call sum function

sum( 10, 20 );

print "Outside the function global total : ", total
```

When the above code is executed, it produces the following result –

Inside the function local total : 30

Outside the function global total : 0

A module allows you to logically organize your Python code. Grouping related code into a module makes the code easier to understand and use. A module is a Python object with arbitrarily named attributes that you can bind and reference.

Simply, a module is a file consisting of Python code. A module can define functions, classes and variables. A module can also include runnable code.

Example

The Python code for a module named aname normally resides in a file named aname.py. Here's an example of a simple module, support.py

```
def print_func( par ):

    print "Hello : ", par

    return
```

The import Statement

You can use any Python source file as a module by executing an import statement in some other Python source file. The import has the following syntax –

```
import module1[, module2[,... moduleN]
```

When the interpreter encounters an import statement, it imports the module if the module is present in the search path. A search path is a list of directories that the interpreter searches before importing a module. For example, to import the module support.py, you need to put the following command at the top of the script –

```
#!/usr/bin/python


# Import module support

import support


# Now you can call defined function that module as follows

support.print_func("Zara")
```

When the above code is executed, it produces the following result –

```
Hello : Zara
```

A module is loaded only once, regardless of the number of times it is imported. This prevents the module execution from happening over and over again if multiple imports occur.

The from...import Statement

Python's from statement lets you import specific attributes from a module into the current namespace. The from...import has the following syntax –

```
from modname import name1[, name2[, ... nameN]]
```

For example, to import the function fibonacci from the module fib, use the following statement –

```
from fib import fibonacci
```

This statement does not import the entire module fib into the current namespace; it just introduces the item fibonacci from the module fib into the global symbol table of the importing module.

The from...import * Statement

It is also possible to import all names from a module into the current namespace by using the following import statement –

```
from modname import *
```

This provides an easy way to import all the items from a module into the current namespace; however, this statement should be used sparingly.

Locating Modules

When you import a module, the Python interpreter searches for the module in the following sequences –

- The current directory.
- If the module isn't found, Python then searches each directory in the shell variable PYTHONPATH.
- If all else fails, Python checks the default path. On UNIX, this default path is normally /usr/local/lib/python/.

The module search path is stored in the system module sys as the sys.pathvariable. The sys.path variable contains the current directory, PYTHONPATH, and the installation-dependent default.

The PYTHONPATH Variable

The PYTHONPATH is an environment variable, consisting of a list of directories. The syntax of PYTHONPATH is the same as that of the shell variable PATH.

Here is a typical PYTHONPATH from a Windows system –

```
set PYTHONPATH = c:\python20\lib;
```

And here is a typical PYTHONPATH from a UNIX system –

```
set PYTHONPATH = /usr/local/lib/python
```

Namespaces and Scoping

Variables are names (identifiers) that map to objects. A namespace is a dictionary of variable names (keys) and their corresponding objects (values).

A Python statement can access variables in a local namespace and in the global namespace. If a local and a global variable have the same name, the local variable shadows the global variable.

Each function has its own local namespace. Class methods follow the same scoping rule as ordinary functions.

Python makes educated guesses on whether variables are local or global. It assumes that any variable assigned a value in a function is local.

Therefore, in order to assign a value to a global variable within a function, you must first use the global statement.

The statement global VarName tells Python that VarName is a global variable. Python stops searching the local namespace for the variable.

For example, we define a variable Money in the global namespace. Within the function Money, we assign Money a value, therefore Python assumes Moneyas a local variable. However, we accessed the value of the local variable Moneybefore setting it, so an UnboundLocalError is the result. Uncommenting the global statement fixes the problem.

```
#!/usr/bin/python


Money = 2000

def AddMoney():

    # Uncomment the following line to fix the code:

    # global Money

    Money = Money + 1


print Money

AddMoney()
```

```
print Money
```

The dir( ) Function

The dir() built-in function returns a sorted list of strings containing the names defined by a module.

The list contains the names of all the modules, variables and functions that are defined in a module. Following is a simple example –

```
#!/usr/bin/python

# Import built-in module math

import math

content = dir(math)

print content
```

When the above code is executed, it produces the following result –

```
['__doc__', '__file__', '__name__', 'acos', 'asin', 'atan',

'atan2', 'ceil', 'cos', 'cosh', 'degrees', 'e', 'exp',

'fabs', 'floor', 'fmod', 'frexp', 'hypot', 'ldexp', 'log',

'log10', 'modf', 'pi', 'pow', 'radians', 'sin', 'sinh',

'sqrt', 'tan', 'tanh']
```

Here, the special string variable __name__ is the module's name, and __file__is the filename from which the module was loaded.

The globals() and locals() Functions

The globals() and locals() functions can be used to return the names in the global and local namespaces depending on the location from where they are called.

If locals() is called from within a function, it will return all the names that can be accessed locally from that function.

If globals() is called from within a function, it will return all the names that can be accessed globally from that function.

The return type of both these functions is dictionary. Therefore, names can be extracted using the keys() function.

The reload() Function

When the module is imported into a script, the code in the top-level portion of a module is executed only once.

Therefore, if you want to reexecute the top-level code in a module, you can use the reload() function. The reload() function imports a previously imported module again. The syntax of the reload() function is this –

```
reload(module_name)
```

Here, module_name is the name of the module you want to reload and not the string containing the module name. For example, to reload hello module, do the following –

```
reload(hello)
```

Packages in Python

A package is a hierarchical file directory structure that defines a single Python application environment that consists of modules and subpackages and sub-subpackages, and so on.

Consider a file Pots.py available in Phone directory. This file has following line of source code –

```
#!/usr/bin/python


def Pots():

   print "I'm Pots Phone"
```

Similar way, we have another two files having different functions with the same name as above –

- Phone/Isdn.py file having function Isdn()
- Phone/G3.py file having function G3()
- Now, create one more file __init__.py in Phone directory –
- Phone/__init__.py

To make all of your functions available when you've imported Phone, you need to put explicit import statements in __init__.py as follows –

```
from Pots import Pots

from Isdn import Isdn

from G3 import G3
```

After you add these lines to __init__.py, you have all of these classes available when you import the Phone package.

```
#!/usr/bin/python


# Now import your Phone Package.

import Phone


Phone.Pots()

Phone.Isdn()

Phone.G3()
```

When the above code is executed, it produces the following result –

```
I'm Pots Phone

I'm 3G Phone

I'm ISDN Phone
```

In the above example, we have taken example of a single functions in each file, but you can keep multiple functions in your files. You can also define different Python classes in those files and then you can create your packages out of those classes.

This chapter covers all the basic I/O functions available in Python. For more functions, please refer to standard Python documentation.

Printing to the Screen

The simplest way to produce output is using the print statement where you can pass zero or more expressions separated by commas. This function converts the expressions you pass into a string and writes the result to standard output as follows –

```
#!/usr/bin/python


print "Python is really a great language,", "isn't it?"
```

This produces the following result on your standard screen –

```
Python is really a great language, isn't it?
```

Reading Keyboard Input

Python provides two built-in functions to read a line of text from standard input, which by default comes from the keyboard. These functions are –

- raw_input
- input

The raw_input Function

The raw_input([prompt]) function reads one line from standard input and returns it as a string (removing the trailing newline).

```
#!/usr/bin/python


str = raw_input("Enter your input: ");

print "Received input is : ", str
```

This prompts you to enter any string and it would display same string on the screen. When I typed "Hello Python!", its output is like this –

```
Enter your input: Hello Python

Received input is :  Hello Python
```

The input Function

The input([prompt]) function is equivalent to raw_input, except that it assumes the input is a valid Python expression and returns the evaluated result to you.

```
#!/usr/bin/python


str = input("Enter your input: ");

print "Received input is : ", str
```

This would produce the following result against the entered input –

```
Enter your input: [x*5 for x in range(2,10,2)]

Recieved input is :  [10, 20, 30, 40]
```

Opening and Closing Files

Until now, you have been reading and writing to the standard input and output. Now, we will see how to use actual data files.

Python provides basic functions and methods necessary to manipulate files by default. You can do most of the file manipulation using a file object.

The open Function

Before you can read or write a file, you have to open it using Python's built-in open() function. This function creates a file object, which would be utilized to call other support methods associated with it.

Syntax

file object = open(file_name [, access_mode][, buffering])

Here are parameter details −

- file_name − The file_name argument is a string value that contains the name of the file that you want to access.

- access_mode − The access_mode determines the mode in which the file has to be opened, i.e., read, write, append, etc. A complete list of possible values is given below in the table. This is optional parameter and the default file access mode is read (r).

- buffering − If the buffering value is set to 0, no buffering takes place. If the buffering value is 1, line buffering is performed while accessing a file. If you specify the buffering value as an integer greater than 1, then buffering action is performed with the indicated buffer size. If negative, the buffer size is the system default(default behavior).

Here is a list of the different modes of opening a file – a new file for reading and writing.

Sr.No.	Modes & Description
1	**r** Opens a file for reading only. The file pointer is placed at the beginning of the file. This is the default mode.
2	**rb** Opens a file for reading only in binary format. The file pointer is placed at the beginning of the file. This is the default mode.
3	**r+** Opens a file for both reading and writing. The file pointer placed at the beginning of the file.
4	**rb+** Opens a file for both reading and writing in binary format. The file pointer placed at the beginning of the file.

5   **w**

Opens a file for writing only. Overwrites the file
if the file exists. If the file does not exist, creates
a new file for writing.

6   **wb**

Opens a file for writing only in binary format.
Overwrites the file if the file exists. If the file
does not exist, creates a new file for writing.

7   **w+**

Opens a file for both writing and reading.
Overwrites the existing file if the file exists. If the
file does not exist, creates a new file for reading
and writing.

8   **wb+**

Opens a file for both writing and reading in
binary format. Overwrites the existing file if the
file exists. If the file does not exist, creates a new
file for reading and writing.

9   **a**

Opens a file for appending. The file pointer is at
the end of the file if the file exists. That is, the
file is in the append mode. If the file does not
exist, it creates a new file for writing.

10 **ab**

Opens a file for appending in binary format. The file pointer is at the end of the file if the file exists. That is, the file is in the append mode. If the file does not exist, it creates a new file for writing.

11 **a+**

Opens a file for both appending and reading. The file pointer is at the end of the file if the file exists. The file opens in the append mode. If the file does not exist, it creates a new file for reading and writing.

12 **ab+**

Opens a file for both appending and reading in binary format. The file pointer is at the end of the file if the file exists. The file opens in the append mode. If the file does not exist, it creates a new file for reading and writing.

The file Object Attributes

Once a file is opened and you have one file object, you can get various information related to that file.

Here is a list of all attributes related to file object –

Sr.No.	Attribute & Description
1	**file.closed** Returns true if file is closed, false otherwise.
2	**file.mode** Returns access mode with which file was opened.
3	**file.name** Returns name of the file.
4	**file.softspace** Returns false if space explicitly required with print, true otherwise.

Example

```
#!/usr/bin/python


# Open a file
```

```
fo = open("foo.txt", "wb")

print "Name of the file: ", fo.name

print "Closed or not : ", fo.closed

print "Opening mode : ", fo.mode

print "Softspace flag : ", fo.softspace
```

This produces the following result –

```
Name of the file:  foo.txt

Closed or not :  False

Opening mode :  wb

Softspace flag :  0
```

The close() Method

The close() method of a file object flushes any unwritten information and closes the file object, after which no more writing can be done.

Python automatically closes a file when the reference object of a file is reassigned to another file. It is a good practice to use the close() method to close a file.

Syntax

```
fileObject.close();
```

Example

```
#!/usr/bin/python
```

```
# Open a file

fo = open("foo.txt", "wb")

print "Name of the file: ", fo.name

# Close opend file

fo.close()
```

This produces the following result –

```
Name of the file:  foo.txt
```

Reading and Writing Files

The file object provides a set of access methods to make our lives easier. We would see how to use read() and write() methods to read and write files.

The write() Method

The write() method writes any string to an open file. It is important to note that Python strings can have binary data and not just text.

The write() method does not add a newline character ('\n') to the end of the string –

Syntax

```
fileObject.write(string);
```

Here, passed parameter is the content to be written into the opened file.

Example

```
#!/usr/bin/python

# Open a file
fo = open("foo.txt", "wb")
fo.write( "Python is a great language.\nYeah its great!!\n");

# Close opend file
fo.close()
```

The above method would create foo.txt file and would write given content in that file and finally it would close that file. If you would open this file, it would have following content.

```
Python is a great language.
Yeah its great!!
```

The read() Method

The read() method reads a string from an open file. It is important to note that Python strings can have binary data. apart from text data.

Syntax

```
fileObject.read([count]);
```

Here, passed parameter is the number of bytes to be read from the opened file. This method starts reading from the beginning of the file and if count is missing, then it tries to read as much as possible, maybe until the end of file.

Example

Let's take a file foo.txt, which we created above.

```
#!/usr/bin/python


# Open a file

fo = open("foo.txt", "r+")

str = fo.read(10);

print "Read String is : ", str

# Close opend file

fo.close()
```

This produces the following result −

```
Read String is :  Python is
```

File Positions

The **tell()** method tells you the current position within the file; in other words, the next read or write will occur at that many bytes from the beginning of the file.

The seek(offset[, from]) method changes the current file position. The offsetargument indicates the number of bytes to be moved. The from argument specifies the reference position from where the bytes are to be moved.

If from is set to 0, it means use the beginning of the file as the reference position and 1 means use the current position as the reference position and if it is set to 2 then the end of the file would be taken as the reference position.

Example

Let us take a file foo.txt, which we created above.

```
#!/usr/bin/python


# Open a file

fo = open("foo.txt", "r+")

str = fo.read(10);

print "Read String is : ", str


# Check current position

position = fo.tell();

print "Current file position : ", position
```

```
# Reposition pointer at the beginning once again

position = fo.seek(0, 0);

str = fo.read(10);

print "Again read String is : ", str

# Close opend file

fo.close()
```

This produces the following result –

```
Read String is :  Python is

Current file position :  10

Again read String is :  Python is
```

Renaming and Deleting Files

Python os module provides methods that help you perform file-processing operations, such as renaming and deleting files.

To use this module you need to import it first and then you can call any related functions.

The rename() Method

The rename() method takes two arguments, the current filename and the new filename.

Syntax:

```
os.rename(current_file_name, new_file_name)
```

Example

Following is the example to rename an existing file test1.txt –

```
#!/usr/bin/python

import os


# Rename a file from test1.txt to test2.txt
os.rename( "test1.txt", "test2.txt" )
```

The remove() Method

You can use the remove() method to delete files by supplying the name of the file to be deleted as the argument.

Syntax

```
os.remove(file_name)
```

Example

Following is the example to delete an existing file test2.txt –

```
#!/usr/bin/python

import os
```

```
# Delete file test2.txt

os.remove("text2.txt")
```

Directories in Python

All files are contained within various directories, and Python has no problem handling these too. The os module has several methods that help you create, remove, and change directories.

The mkdir() Method

You can use the *mkdir()* method of the os module to create directories in the current directory. You need to supply an argument to this method which contains the name of the directory to be created.

Syntax

```
os.mkdir("newdir")
```

Example

Following is the example to create a directory test in the current directory –

```
#!/usr/bin/python

import os


# Create a directory "test"

os.mkdir("test")
```

The chdir() Method

You can use the chdir() method to change the current directory. The chdir() method takes an argument, which is the name of the directory that you want to make the current directory.

Syntax

```
os.chdir("newdir")
```

Example

Following is the example to go into "/home/newdir" directory −

```
#!/usr/bin/python

import os


# Changing a directory to "/home/newdir"

os.chdir("/home/newdir")
```

The getcwd() Method

The getcwd() method displays the current working directory.

Syntax

```
os.getcwd()
```

Example

Following is the example to give current directory −

```
#!/usr/bin/python

import os


# This would give location of the current directory

os.getcwd()
```

The rmdir() Method

The rmdir() method deletes the directory, which is passed as an argument in the method.

Before removing a directory, all the contents in it should be removed.

Syntax

```
os.rmdir('dirname')
```

Example

Following is the example to remove "/tmp/test" directory. It is required to give fully qualified name of the directory, otherwise it would search for that directory in the current directory.

```
import os


# This would  remove "/tmp/test"  directory.

os.rmdir( "/tmp/test"  )
```

File & Directory Related Methods

There are three important sources, which provide a wide range of utility methods to handle and manipulate files & directories on Windows and Unix operating systems. They are as follows −

- File Object Methods: The file object provides functions to manipulate files.

- OS Object Methods: This provides methods to process files as well as directories.

- Python provides two very important features to handle any unexpected error in your Python programs and to add debugging capabilities in them −

- Exception Handling − This would be covered in this tutorial. Here is a list standard Exceptions available in Python: Standard Exceptions.

- Assertions − This would be covered in Assertions in Pythontutorial.

List of Standard Exceptions −

Sr.No.	Exception Name & Description
1	**Exception** Base class for all exceptions
2	**StopIteration** Raised when the next() method of an iterator does not point to any object.

| 3 | **SystemExit** |
| | Raised by the sys.exit() function. |

| 4 | **StandardError** |
| | Base class for all built-in exceptions except StopIteration and SystemExit. |

| 5 | **ArithmeticError** |
| | Base class for all errors that occur for numeric calculation. |

| 6 | **OverflowError** |
| | Raised when a calculation exceeds maximum limit for a numeric type. |

| 7 | **FloatingPointError** |
| | Raised when a floating point calculation fails. |

| 8 | **ZeroDivisionError** |
| | Raised when division or modulo by zero takes place for all numeric types. |

| 9 | **AssertionError** |
| | Raised in case of failure of the Assert statement. |

10   **AttributeError**

Raised in case of failure of attribute reference or assignment.

11   **EOFError**

Raised when there is no input from either the raw_input() or input() function and the end of file is reached.

12   **ImportError**

Raised when an import statement fails.

13   **KeyboardInterrupt**

Raised when the user interrupts program execution, usually by pressing Ctrl+c.

14   **LookupError**

Base class for all lookup errors.

15   **IndexError**

Raised when an index is not found in a sequence.

16   **KeyError**

Raised when the specified key is not found in the dictionary.

17   **NameError**

Raised when an identifier is not found in the local or global namespace.

18   **UnboundLocalError**

Raised when trying to access a local variable in a function or method but no value has been assigned to it.

19   **EnvironmentError**

Base class for all exceptions that occur outside the Python environment.

20   **IOError**

Raised when an input/ output operation fails, such as the print statement or the open() function when trying to open a file that does not exist.

21   **IOError**

Raised for operating system-related errors.

22   **SyntaxError**

Raised when there is an error in Python syntax.

23   **IndentationError**

Raised when indentation is not specified properly.

24   SystemError

Raised when the interpreter finds an internal problem, but when this error is encountered the Python interpreter does not exit.

25   SystemExit

Raised when Python interpreter is quit by using the sys.exit() function. If not handled in the code, causes the interpreter to exit.

26   TypeError

Raised when an operation or function is attempted that is invalid for the specified data type.

27   ValueError

Raised when the built-in function for a data type has the valid type of arguments, but the arguments have invalid values specified.

28   RuntimeError

Raised when a generated error does not fall into any category.

29   NotImplementedError

Raised when an abstract method that needs to be implemented in an inherited class is not actually implemented.

Raised when an abstract method that needs to be implemented in an inherited class is not actually implemented.

Assertions in Python

An assertion is a sanity-check that you can turn on or turn off when you are done with your testing of the program.

The easiest way to think of an assertion is to liken it to a raise-if statement (or to be more accurate, a raise-if-not statement). An expression is tested, and if the result comes up false, an exception is raised.

Assertions are carried out by the assert statement, the newest keyword to Python, introduced in version 1.5.

Programmers often place assertions at the start of a function to check for valid input, and after a function call to check for valid output.

The assert Statement

When it encounters an assert statement, Python evaluates the accompanying expression, which is hopefully true. If the expression is false, Python raises an AssertionError exception.

The syntax for assert is –

```
assert Expression[, Arguments]
```

If the assertion fails, Python uses ArgumentExpression as the argument for the AssertionError. AssertionError exceptions can be caught and handled like any other exception using the try-except statement, but if not handled, they will terminate the program and produce a traceback.

Example

Here is a function that converts a temperature from degrees Kelvin to degrees Fahrenheit. Since zero degrees Kelvin is as cold as it gets, the function bails out if it sees a negative temperature –

```
#!/usr/bin/python

def KelvinToFahrenheit(Temperature):

   assert (Temperature >= 0),"Colder than absolute zero!"

   return ((Temperature-273)*1.8)+32

print KelvinToFahrenheit(273)

print int(KelvinToFahrenheit(505.78))
```

print KelvinToFahrenheit

When the above code is executed, it produces the following result –

```
32.0

451

Traceback (most recent call last):

File "test.py", line 9, in <module>

print KelvinToFahrenheit(-5)

File "test.py", line 4, in KelvinToFahrenheit

assert (Temperature >= 0),"Colder than absolute zero!"

AssertionError: Colder than absolute zero!
```

What is Exception?

An exception is an event, which occurs during the execution of a program that disrupts the normal flow of the program's instructions. In general, when a Python script encounters a situation that it cannot cope with, it raises an exception. An exception is a Python object that represents an error.

When a Python script raises an exception, it must either handle the exception immediately otherwise it terminates and quits.

Handling an exception

If you have some suspicious code that may raise an exception, you can defend your program by placing the suspicious code in a try: block. After the try: block, include an except: statement, followed by a block of code which handles the problem as elegantly as possible.

Syntax

Here is simple syntax of try....except...else blocks –

```
try:
   You do your operations here;
   ....................
except ExceptionI:
   If there is ExceptionI, then execute this block.
except ExceptionII:
   If there is ExceptionII, then execute this block.
```

....

else:

If there is no exception then execute this block.

Here are few important points about the above-mentioned syntax –

- A single try statement can have multiple except statements. This is useful when the try block contains statements that may throw different types of exceptions.

- You can also provide a generic except clause, which handles any exception.

- After the except clause(s), you can include an else-clause. The code in the else-block executes if the code in the try: block does not raise an exception.

- The else-block is a good place for code that does not need the try: block's protection.

Example

This example opens a file, writes content in the, file and comes out gracefully because there is no problem at all –

```
#!/usr/bin/python


try:

    fh = open("testfile", "w")

    fh.write("This is my test file for exception handling!!")
```

```
except IOError:

    print "Error: can\'t find file or read data"

else:

    print "Written content in the file successfully"

fh.close()
```

This produces the following result −

```
Written content in the file successfully
```

Example

This example tries to open a file where you do not have write permission, so it raises an exception −

```
#!/usr/bin/python


try:

    fh = open("testfile", "r")

    fh.write("This is my test file for exception handling!!")

except IOError:

    print "Error: can\'t find file or read data"

else:

    print "Written content in the file successfully"
```

This produces the following result −

```
Error: can't find file or read data
```

The except Clause with No Exceptions

You can also use the except statement with no exceptions defined as follows –

```
try:

   You do your operations here;

   ........................

except:

   If there is any exception, then execute this block.

   ........................

else:

   If there is no exception then execute this block.
```

This kind of a try-except statement catches all the exceptions that occur. Using this kind of try-except statement is not considered a good programming practice though, because it catches all exceptions but does not make the programmer identify the root cause of the problem that may occur.

The except Clause with Multiple Exceptions

You can also use the same except statement to handle multiple exceptions as follows –

```
try:

   You do your operations here;

   ........................

except(Exception1[, Exception2[,...ExceptionN]]]):
```

If there is any exception from the given exception list,

then execute this block.

....

else:

If there is no exception then execute this block.

The try-finally Clause

You can use a finally: block along with a try: block. The finally block is a place to put any code that must execute, whether the try-block raised an exception or not. The syntax of the try-finally statement is this –

try:

You do your operations here;

....

Due to any exception, this may be skipped.

finally:

This would always be executed.

....

You cannot use else clause as well along with a finally clause.

Example

```
#!/usr/bin/python
```

```
try:

   fh = open("testfile", "w")

   fh.write("This is my test file for exception handling!!")

finally:

   print "Error: can\'t find file or read data"
```

If you do not have permission to open the file in writing mode, then this will produce the following result –

```
Error: can't find file or read data
```

Same example can be written more cleanly as follows –

```
#!/usr/bin/python


try:

   fh = open("testfile", "w")

   try:

      fh.write("This is my test file for exception handling!!")

   finally:

      print "Going to close the file"

      fh.close()

except IOError:

   print "Error: can\'t find file or read data"
```

When an exception is thrown in the try block, the execution immediately passes to the finally block. After all the statements in the finally block are executed, the exception is raised again and is handled in the exceptstatements if present in the next higher layer of the try-except statement.

Argument of an Exception

An exception can have an argument, which is a value that gives additional information about the problem. The contents of the argument vary by exception. You capture an exception's argument by supplying a variable in the except clause as follows –

```
try:

   You do your operations here;

   .....................

except ExceptionType, Argument:

   You can print value of Argument here...
```

If you write the code to handle a single exception, you can have a variable follow the name of the exception in the except statement. If you are trapping multiple exceptions, you can have a variable follow the tuple of the exception.

This variable receives the value of the exception mostly containing the cause of the exception. The variable can receive a single value or multiple values in the form of a tuple. This tuple usually contains the error string, the error number, and an error location.

Example

Following is an example for a single exception –

```
#!/usr/bin/python


# Define a function here.

def temp_convert(var):

   try:

      return int(var)

   except ValueError, Argument:

      print "The argument does not contain numbers\n",
Argument

# Call above function here.

temp_convert("xyz");
```

This produces the following result –

The argument does not contain numbers

invalid literal for int() with base 10: 'xyz'

Raising an Exceptions

You can raise exceptions in several ways by using the raise statement. The general syntax for the raise statement is as follows.

Syntax

```
raise [Exception [, args [, traceback]]]
```

Here, Exception is the type of exception (for example, NameError) and argument is a value for the exception argument. The argument is optional; if not supplied, the exception argument is None.

The final argument, traceback, is also optional (and rarely used in practice), and if present, is the traceback object used for the exception.

Example

An exception can be a string, a class or an object. Most of the exceptions that the Python core raises are classes, with an argument that is an instance of the class. Defining new exceptions is quite easy and can be done as follows –

```
def functionName( level ):

  if level < 1:

    raise "Invalid level!", level

    # The code below to this would not be executed

    # if we raise the exception
```

Note: In order to catch an exception, an "except" clause must refer to the same exception thrown either class object or simple string. For example, to capture above exception, we must write the except clause as follows –

```
try:

  Business Logic here...

except "Invalid level!":

  Exception handling here...

else:
```

Rest of the code here...

User-Defined Exceptions

Python also allows you to create your own exceptions by deriving classes from the standard built-in exceptions.

Here is an example related to RuntimeError. Here, a class is created that is subclassed from RuntimeError. This is useful when you need to display more specific information when an exception is caught.

In the try block, the user-defined exception is raised and caught in the except block. The variable e is used to create an instance of the class Networkerror.

```
class Networkerror(RuntimeError):

    def __init__(self, arg):

        self.args = arg
```

So once you defined above class, you can raise the exception as follows –

```
try:

    raise Networkerror("Bad hostname")

except Networkerror,e:

    print e.args
```

OBJECT-ORIENTED PROGRAMMING

Python has been an object-oriented language since it existed. Because of this, creating and using classes and objects are downright easy. This chapter helps you become an expert in using Python's object-oriented programming support.

If you do not have any previous experience with object-oriented (OO) programming, you may want to consult an introductory course on it or at least a tutorial of some sort so that you have a grasp of the basic concepts.

However, here is small introduction of Object-Oriented Programming (OOP) to bring you at speed –

Overview of OOP Terminology

- Class – A user-defined prototype for an object that defines a set of attributes that characterize any object of the class. The attributes are data members (class variables and instance variables) and methods, accessed via dot notation.

- Class variable – A variable that is shared by all instances of a class. Class variables are defined within a class but outside any of the class's methods. Class variables are not used as frequently as instance variables are.

- Data member – A class variable or instance variable that holds data associated with a class and its objects.

- Function overloading – The assignment of more than one behavior to a particular function. The operation performed varies by the types of objects or arguments involved.

- Instance variable – A variable that is defined inside a method and belongs only to the current instance of a class.

- Inheritance – The transfer of the characteristics of a class to other classes that are derived from it.

- Instance – An individual object of a certain class. An object obj that belongs to a class Circle, for example, is an instance of the class Circle.

- Instantiation – The creation of an instance of a class.

- Method – A special kind of function that is defined in a class definition.

- Object – A unique instance of a data structure that's defined by its class. An object comprises both data members (class variables and instance variables) and methods.

- Operator overloading – The assignment of more than one function to a particular operator.

Creating Classes

The class statement creates a new class definition. The name of the class immediately follows the keyword class followed by a colon as follows –

```
class ClassName:
    'Optional class documentation string'
    class_suite
```

- The class has a documentation string, which can be accessed via ClassName.__doc__.

- The class_suite consists of all the component statements defining class members, data attributes and functions.

Example

Following is the example of a simple Python class –

```
class Employee:
  'Common base class for all employees'
  empCount = 0


  def __init__(self, name, salary):
    self.name = name
    self.salary = salary
    Employee.empCount += 1


  def displayCount(self):
    print "Total Employee %d" % Employee.empCount


  def displayEmployee(self):
    print "Name : ", self.name,  ", Salary: ", self.salary
```

- The variable empCount is a class variable whose value is shared among all instances of a this class. This can be accessed as

Employee.empCount from inside the class or outside the class.

- The first method __init__() is a special method, which is called class constructor or initialization method that Python calls when you create a new instance of this class.

- You declare other class methods like normal functions with the exception that the first argument to each method is self. Python adds the self argument to the list for you; you do not need to include it when you call the methods.

Creating Instance Objects

To create instances of a class, you call the class using class name and pass in whatever arguments its __init__ method accepts.

"This would create first object of Employee class"

emp1 = Employee("Zara", 2000)

"This would create second object of Employee class"

emp2 = Employee("Manni", 5000)

Accessing Attributes

You access the object's attributes using the dot operator with object. Class variable would be accessed using class name as follows −

emp1.displayEmployee()

emp2.displayEmployee()

print "Total Employee %d" % Employee.empCount

Now, putting all the concepts together –

```
#!/usr/bin/python

class Employee:
  'Common base class for all employees'
  empCount = 0

  def __init__(self, name, salary):
    self.name = name
    self.salary = salary
    Employee.empCount += 1

  def displayCount(self):
    print "Total Employee %d" % Employee.empCount

  def displayEmployee(self):
    print "Name : ", self.name,  ", Salary: ", self.salary

"This would create first object of Employee class"
emp1 = Employee("Zara", 2000)
"This would create second object of Employee class"
```

```
emp2 = Employee("Manni", 5000)

emp1.displayEmployee()

emp2.displayEmployee()

print "Total Employee %d" % Employee.empCount
```

When the above code is executed, it produces the following result –

```
Name : Zara ,Salary: 2000

Name : Manni ,Salary: 5000

Total Employee 2
```

You can add, remove, or modify attributes of classes and objects at any time –

```
emp1.age = 7  # Add an 'age' attribute.

emp1.age = 8  # Modify 'age' attribute.

del emp1.age  # Delete 'age' attribute.
```

Instead of using the normal statements to access attributes, you can use the following functions –

- The getattr(obj, name[, default]) – to access the attribute of object.
- The hasattr(obj,name) – to check if an attribute exists or not.
- The setattr(obj,name,value) – to set an attribute. If attribute does not exist, then it would be created.
- The delattr(obj, name) – to delete an attribute.

```
hasattr(emp1, 'age')    # Returns true if 'age' attribute exists
```

```
getattr(emp1, 'age')    # Returns value of 'age' attribute

setattr(emp1, 'age', 8) # Set attribute 'age' at 8

delattr(empl, 'age')    # Delete attribute 'age'
```

Built-In Class Attributes

Every Python class keeps following built-in attributes and they can be accessed using dot operator like any other attribute –

- __dict__ – Dictionary containing the class's namespace.

- __doc__ – Class documentation string or none, if undefined.

- __name__ – Class name.

- __module__ – Module name in which the class is defined. This attribute is "__main__" in interactive mode.

- __bases__ – A possibly empty tuple containing the base classes, in the order of their occurrence in the base class list.

For the above class let us try to access all these attributes –

```
#!/usr/bin/python


class Employee:

   'Common base class for all employees'

   empCount = 0
```

```
def __init__(self, name, salary):

    self.name = name

    self.salary = salary

    Employee.empCount += 1


def displayCount(self):

    print "Total Employee %d" % Employee.empCount


def displayEmployee(self):

    print "Name : ", self.name,  ", Salary: ", self.salary


print "Employee.__doc__:", Employee.__doc__

print "Employee.__name__:", Employee.__name__

print "Employee.__module__:", Employee.__module__

print "Employee.__bases__:", Employee.__bases__

print "Employee.__dict__:", Employee.__dict__
```

When the above code is executed, it produces the following result –

```
Employee.__doc__: Common base class for all employees

Employee.__name__: Employee

Employee.__module__: __main__
```

Employee.__bases__: ()

Employee.__dict__: {'__module__': '__main__', 'displayCount':

<function displayCount at 0xb7c84994>, 'empCount': 2,

'displayEmployee':   <function   displayEmployee   at
0xb7c8441c>,

'__doc__': 'Common base class for all employees',

'__init__': <function __init__ at 0xb7c846bc>}

Destroying Objects (Garbage Collection)

Python deletes unneeded objects (built-in types or class instances) automatically to free the memory space. The process by which Python periodically reclaims blocks of memory that no longer are in use is termed Garbage Collection.

Python's garbage collector runs during program execution and is triggered when an object's reference count reaches zero. An object's reference count changes as the number of aliases that point to it changes.

An object's reference count increases when it is assigned a new name or placed in a container (list, tuple, or dictionary). The object's reference count decreases when it's deleted with del, its reference is reassigned, or its reference goes out of scope. When an object's reference count reaches zero, Python collects it automatically.

```
a = 40      # Create object <40>

b = a       # Increase ref. count  of <40>

c = [b]     # Increase ref. count  of <40>
```

```
del a      # Decrease ref. count  of <40>

b = 100    # Decrease ref. count  of <40>

c[0] = -1  # Decrease ref. count  of <40>
```

You normally will not notice when the garbage collector destroys an orphaned instance and reclaims its space. But a class can implement the special method __del__(), called a destructor, that is invoked when the instance is about to be destroyed. This method might be used to clean up any non memory resources used by an instance.

Example

This __del__() destructor prints the class name of an instance that is about to be destroyed –

```
#!/usr/bin/python


class Point:
   def __init__( self, x=0, y=0):
      self.x = x
      self.y = y
   def __del__(self):
      class_name = self.__class__.__name__
      print class_name, "destroyed"


pt1 = Point()
```

```
pt2 = pt1

pt3 = pt1

print id(pt1), id(pt2), id(pt3) # prints the ids of the obejcts

del pt1

del pt2

del pt3
```

When the above code is executed, it produces following result −

```
3083401324 3083401324 3083401324

Point destroyed
```

Note − Ideally, you should define your classes in separate file, then you should import them in your main program file using import statement.

Class Inheritance

Instead of starting from scratch, you can create a class by deriving it from a preexisting class by listing the parent class in parentheses after the new class name.

The child class inherits the attributes of its parent class, and you can use those attributes as if they were defined in the child class. A child class can also override data members and methods from the parent.

Syntax

Derived classes are declared much like their parent class; however, a list of base classes to inherit from is given after the class name −

```
class SubClassName (ParentClass1[, ParentClass2, ...]):
   'Optional class documentation string'
   class_suite
```

Example

```
#!/usr/bin/python

class Parent:        # define parent class
   parentAttr = 100
   def __init__(self):
      print "Calling parent constructor"

   def parentMethod(self):
      print 'Calling parent method'

   def setAttr(self, attr):
      Parent.parentAttr = attr

   def getAttr(self):
      print "Parent attribute :", Parent.parentAttr

class Child(Parent): # define child class
```

```
    def __init__(self):

        print "Calling child constructor"


    def childMethod(self):

        print 'Calling child method'


c = Child()          # instance of child

c.childMethod()        # child calls its method

c.parentMethod()       # calls parent's method

c.setAttr(200)         # again call parent's method

c.getAttr()            # again call parent's method
```

When the above code is executed, it produces the following result –

```
Calling child constructor
Calling child method
Calling parent method
Parent attribute : 200
```

Similar way, you can drive a class from multiple parent classes as follows –

```
class A:        # define your class A

.....


class B:        # define your class B
```

```
.....

class C(A, B):   # subclass of A and B

.....
```

You can use issubclass() or isinstance() functions to check a relationships of two classes and instances.

- The issubclass(sub, sup) boolean function returns true if the given subclass sub is indeed a subclass of the superclass sup.

- The isinstance(obj, Class) boolean function returns true if obj is an instance of class Class or is an instance of a subclass of Class

Overriding Methods

You can always override your parent class methods. One reason for overriding parent's methods is because you may want special or different functionality in your subclass.

Example

```
#!/usr/bin/python

class Parent:      # define parent class

  def myMethod(self):

    print 'Calling parent method'
```

```
class Child(Parent): # define child class

  def myMethod(self):

    print 'Calling child method'


c = Child()        # instance of child

c.myMethod()       # child calls overridden method
```

When the above code is executed, it produces the following result −

```
Calling child method
```

Base Overloading Methods

Following table lists some generic functionality that you can override in your own classes −

Sr.No.	Method, Description & Sample Call
1	**__init__ (self [,args...])** Constructor (with any optional arguments) Sample Call : *obj = className(args)*
2	**__del__(self)** Destructor, deletes an object

Sample Call : *del obj*

3   **__repr__(self)**

Evaluable string representation

Sample Call : *repr(obj)*

4   **__str__(self)**

Printable string representation

Sample Call : *str(obj)*

5   **__cmp__ (self, x)**

Object comparison

Sample Call : *cmp(obj, x)*

Overloading Operators

Suppose you have created a Vector class to represent two-dimensional vectors, what happens when you use the plus operator to add them? Most likely Python will yell at you.

You could, however, define the __add__ method in your class to perform vector addition and then the plus operator would behave as per expectation –

Example

```
#!/usr/bin/python


class Vector:
  def __init__(self, a, b):
    self.a = a
    self.b = b


  def __str__(self):
    return 'Vector (%d, %d)' % (self.a, self.b)


  def __add__(self,other):
    return Vector(self.a + other.a, self.b + other.b)


v1 = Vector(2,10)
v2 = Vector(5,-2)
print v1 + v2
```

When the above code is executed, it produces the following result −

```
Vector(7,8)
```

Data Hiding

An object's attributes may or may not be visible outside the class definition. You need to name attributes with a double underscore prefix, and those attributes then are not be directly visible to outsiders.

```
#!/usr/bin/python


class JustCounter:

   __secretCount = 0


   def count(self):

      self.__secretCount += 1

      print self.__secretCount


counter = JustCounter()

counter.count()

counter.count()

print counter.__secretCount
```

When the above code is executed, it produces the following result –

```
1
2
Traceback (most recent call last):
```

```
File "test.py", line 12, in <module>

    print counter.__secretCount
```

AttributeError: JustCounter instance has no attribute '__secretCount'

Python protects those members by internally changing the name to include the class name. You can access such attributes as object._className__attrName. If you would replace your last line as following, then it works for you –

```
.........................
```

print counter._JustCounter__secretCount

When the above code is executed, it produces the following result –

```
1
2
2
```

REGULAR EXPRESSIONS

A *regular expression* is a special sequence of characters that helps you match or find other strings or sets of strings, using a specialized syntax held in a pattern. Regular expressions are widely used in UNIX world.

The module re provides full support for Perl-like regular expressions in Python. The re module raises the exception re.error if an error occurs while compiling or using a regular expression.

We would cover two important functions, which would be used to handle regular expressions. But a small thing first: There are various characters, which would have special meaning when they are used in regular expression. To avoid any confusion while dealing with regular expressions, we would use Raw Strings as r'expression'.

The match Function

This function attempts to match RE pattern to string with optional flags.

Here is the syntax for this function –

re.match(pattern, string, flags=0)

Here is the description of the parameters –

Sr.No.	Parameter & Description
1	**pattern** This is the regular expression to be matched.
2	**string** This is the string, which would be searched to match the pattern at the beginning of string.
3	**flags** You can specify different flags using bitwise OR (|). These are modifiers, which are listed in the table below.

The re.match function returns a match object on success, None on failure. We usegroup(num) or groups() function of match object to get matched expression.

Sr.No.	Match Object Method & Description
1	**group(num=0)** This method returns entire match (or specific subgroup num)
2	**groups()** This method returns all matching subgroups in a tuple (empty if there weren't any)

This method returns all matching subgroups in a tuple (empty if there weren't any)

Example

```
#!/usr/bin/python

import re

line = "Cats are smarter than dogs"

matchObj = re.match( r'(.*) are (.*?) .*', line, re.M|re.I)


if matchObj:

   print "matchObj.group() : ", matchObj.group()

   print "matchObj.group(1) : ", matchObj.group(1)

   print "matchObj.group(2) : ", matchObj.group(2)
```

```
else:

  print "No match!!"
```

When the above code is executed, it produces following result −

```
matchObj.group() :  Cats are smarter than dogs

matchObj.group(1) :  Cats

matchObj.group(2) :  smarter
```

The search Function

This function searches for first occurrence of RE pattern within string with optional flags.

Here is the syntax for this function −

```
re.search(pattern, string, flags=0)
```

Here is the description of the parameters −

Sr.No.	Parameter & Description
1	**pattern** This is the regular expression to be matched.
2	**string** This is the string, which would be searched to match the pattern anywhere in the string.

3	**flags**
	You can specify different flags using bitwise OR (|). These are modifiers, which are listed in the table below.

The re.search function returns a match object on success, none on failure. We use group(num) or groups() function of match object to get matched expression.

Sr.No.	Match Object Methods & Description
1	**group(num=0)**
	This method returns entire match (or specific subgroup num)
2	**groups()**
	This method returns all matching subgroups in a tuple (empty if there weren't any)

Example

```
#!/usr/bin/python

import re


line = "Cats are smarter than dogs";
```

```
searchObj = re.search( r'(.*) are (.*?) .*', line, re.M | re.I)

if searchObj:

    print "searchObj.group() : ", searchObj.group()

    print "searchObj.group(1) : ", searchObj.group(1)

    print "searchObj.group(2) : ", searchObj.group(2)

else:

    print "Nothing found!!"
```

When the above code is executed, it produces following result –

```
searchObj.group() :  Cats are smarter than dogs
searchObj.group(1) :  Cats
searchObj.group(2) :  smarter
```

Matching Versus Searching

Python offers two different primitive operations based on regular expressions: match checks for a match only at the beginning of the string, while searchchecks for a match anywhere in the string (this is what Perl does by default).

Example

```
#!/usr/bin/python

import re


line = "Cats are smarter than dogs";


matchObj = re.match( r'dogs', line, re.M|re.I)
if matchObj:
   print "match --> matchObj.group() : ", matchObj.group()
else:
   print "No match!!"


searchObj = re.search( r'dogs', line, re.M|re.I)
if searchObj:
   print "search --> searchObj.group() : ", searchObj.group()
else:
   print "Nothing found!!"
```

When the above code is executed, it produces the
following result –

```
No match!!
search --> matchObj.group() :  dogs
```

Search and Replace

One of the most important re methods that use regular expressions is sub.

Syntax

e.sub(pattern, repl, string, max=0)

This method replaces all occurrences of the RE pattern in string with repl, substituting all occurrences unless max provided. This method returns modified string.

Example

```
#!/usr/bin/python

import re


phone = "2004-959-559 # This is Phone Number"


# Delete Python-style comments

num = re.sub(r'#.*$', "", phone)

print "Phone Num : ", num


# Remove anything other than digits

num = re.sub(r'\D', "", phone)

print "Phone Num : ", num
```

When the above code is executed, it produces the following result –

Phone Num : 2004-959-559

Phone Num : 2004959559

Regular Expression Modifiers: Option Flags

Regular expression literals may include an optional modifier to control various aspects of matching. The modifiers are specified as an optional flag. You can provide multiple modifiers using exclusive OR (|), as shown previously and may be represented by one of these −

Sr.No.	Modifier & Description
1	**re.I** Performs case-insensitive matching.
2	**re.L** Interprets words according to the current locale. This interpretation affects the alphabetic group (\w and \W), as well as word boundary behavior(\b and \B).
3	**re.M** Makes $ match the end of a line (not just the end of the string) and makes ^ match the start of any line (not just the start of the string).

4	**re.S**
	Makes a period (dot) match any character, including a newline.
5	**re.U**
	Interprets letters according to the Unicode character set. This flag affects the behavior of \w, \W, \b, \B.
6	**re.X**
	Permits "cuter" regular expression syntax. It ignores whitespace (except inside a set [] or when escaped by a backslash) and treats unescaped # as a comment marker.

Regular Expression Patterns

Except for control characters, (+ ? . * ^ $ ( ) [ ] { } | \), all characters match themselves. You can escape a control character by preceding it with a backslash.

Following table lists the regular expression syntax that is available in Python –

Sr.No.	Pattern & Description

| 1 | **^**

Matches beginning of line. |

1

^

Matches beginning of line.

2

$

Matches end of line.

3

.

Matches any single character except newline. Using m option allows it to match newline as well.

4

[...]

Matches any single character in brackets.

5

[^...]

Matches any single character not in brackets

6

re*

Matches 0 or more occurrences of preceding expression.

7

re+

Matches 1 or more occurrence of preceding expression.

8

re?

Matches 0 or 1 occurrence of preceding expression.

9

re{ n}

Matches exactly n number of occurrences of
preceding expression.

10

re{ n,}

Matches n or more occurrences of preceding
expression.

11

re{ n, m}

Matches at least n and at most m occurrences
of preceding expression.

12

a| b

Matches either a or b.

13

(re)

Groups regular expressions and remembers
matched text.

14

(?imx)

Temporarily toggles on i, m, or x options
within a regular expression. If in parentheses,
only that area is affected.

15

(?-imx)

Temporarily toggles off i, m, or x options
within a regular expression. If in parentheses,
only that area is affected.

16

(?: re)

Groups regular expressions without remembering matched text.

(?imx: re)

17

Temporarily toggles on i, m, or x options within parentheses.

(?-imx: re)

18

Temporarily toggles off i, m, or x options within parentheses.

(?#...)

19

Comment.

(?= re)

20

Specifies position using a pattern. Doesn't have a range.

(?! re)

21

Specifies position using pattern negation. Doesn't have a range.

(?> re)

22

Matches independent pattern without backtracking.

\w

23

Matches word characters.

| 24 | **\W** |
| | Matches nonword characters. |

| 25 | **\s** |
| | Matches whitespace. Equivalent to [\t\n\r\f]. |

| 26 | **\S** |
| | Matches nonwhitespace. |

| 27 | **\d** |
| | Matches digits. Equivalent to [0-9]. |

| 28 | **\D** |
| | Matches nondigits. |

| 29 | **\A** |
| | Matches beginning of string. |

| 30 | **\Z** |
| | Matches end of string. If a newline exists, it matches just before newline. |

| 31 | **\z** |
| | Matches end of string. |

| 32 | **\G** |
| | Matches point where last match finished. |

33

\b

Matches word boundaries when outside brackets. Matches backspace (0x08) when inside brackets.

34

\B

Matches nonword boundaries.

35

\n, \t, etc.

Matches newlines, carriage returns, tabs, etc.

36

\1...\9

Matches nth grouped subexpression.

37

\10

Matches nth grouped subexpression if it matched already. Otherwise refers to the octal representation of a character code.

Regular Expression Examples

Literal characters

Sr.No.	Example & Description
1	**python** Match "python".

Character classes

Sr.No.	Example & Description
1	**[Pp]ython** Match "Python" or "python"
2	**rub[ye]** Match "ruby" or "rube"
3	**[aeiou]** Match any one lowercase vowel
4	**[0-9]** Match any digit; same as [0123456789]
5	**[a-z]** Match any lowercase ASCII letter

6	**[A-Z]**
	Match any uppercase ASCII letter

7	**[a-zA-Z0-9]**
	Match any of the above

8	**[^aeiou]**
	Match anything other than a lowercase vowel

9	**[^0-9]**
	Match anything other than a digit

Special Character Classes

Sr.No.	Example & Description
1	.
	Match any character except newline
2	**\d**
	Match a digit: [0-9]
3	**\D**
	Match a nondigit: [^0-9]
4	**\s**
	Match a whitespace character: [\t\r\n\f]

5	**\S** Match nonwhitespace: [^ \t\r\n\f]
6	**\w** Match a single word character: [A-Za-z0-9_]
7	**\W** Match a nonword character: [^A-Za-z0-9_]

Repetition Cases

Sr.No.	Example & Description
1	**ruby?** Match "rub" or "ruby": the y is optional
2	**ruby*** Match "rub" plus 0 or more ys
3	**ruby+** Match "rub" plus 1 or more ys
4	**\d{3}** Match exactly 3 digits
5	**\d{3,}**

	Match 3 or more digits
6	**\d{3,5}** Match 3, 4, or 5 digits

Nongreedy repetition

This matches the smallest number of repetitions –

Sr.No.	Example & Description
1	**<.*>** Greedy repetition: matches "<python>perl>"
2	**<.*?>** Nongreedy: matches "<python>" in "<python>perl>"

Grouping with Parentheses

Sr.No.	Example & Description
1	**\D\d+** No group: + repeats \d

2	**(\D\d)+**
	Grouped: + repeats \D\d pair

3	**([Pp]ython(,)?)+**
	Match "Python", "Python, python, python", etc.

Backreferences

Sr.No.	Example & Description
1	**([Pp])ython&\1ails**
	Match python&pails or Python&Pails
2	**(["'])[^\1]*\1**
	Single or double-quoted string. \1 matches whatever the 1st group matched. \2 matches whatever the 2nd group matched, etc.

Alternatives

Sr.No.	Example & Description
1	**python|perl**
	Match "python" or "perl"
2	**rub(y|le))**

Match "ruby" or "ruble"

Python(!+ | \?)

3

"Python" followed by one or more ! or one ?

Anchors

This needs to specify match position.

Sr.No.	Example & Description
1	**^Python** Match "Python" at the start of a string or internal line
2	**Python$** Match "Python" at the end of a string or line
3	**\APython** Match "Python" at the start of a string
4	**Python\Z** Match "Python" at the end of a string
5	**\bPython\b** Match "Python" at a word boundary
6	**\brub\B**

\B is nonword boundary: match "rub" in "rube" and "ruby" but not alone

7

Python(?=!)

Match "Python", if followed by an exclamation point.

8

Python(?!!)

Match "Python", if not followed by an exclamation point.

Special Syntax with Parentheses

Sr.No.	Example & Description
1	**R(?#comment)** Matches "R". All the rest is a comment
2	**R(?i)uby** Case-insensitive while matching "uby"
3	**R(?i:uby)** Same as above
4	**rub(?:y|le))** Group only without creating \1 backreference

PYTHON - CGI PROGRAMMING

The Common Gateway Interface, or CGI, is a set of standards that define how information is exchanged between the web server and a custom script. The CGI specs are currently maintained by the NCSA.

What is CGI?

- The Common Gateway Interface, or CGI, is a standard for external gateway programs to interface with information servers such as HTTP servers.

- The current version is CGI/1.1 and CGI/1.2 is under progress.

Web Browsing

To understand the concept of CGI, let us see what happens when we click a hyper link to browse a particular web page or URL.

- Your browser contacts the HTTP web server and demands for the URL, i.e., filename.

- Web Server parses the URL and looks for the filename. If it finds that file then sends it back to the browser, otherwise sends an error message indicating that you requested a wrong file.

- Web browser takes response from web server and displays either the received file or error message.

However, it is possible to set up the HTTP server so that whenever a file in a certain directory is requested that file is not sent back; instead it is executed as a program, and whatever that program outputs is sent back for your browser to display. This function is called the Common Gateway Interface or CGI and the programs are called CGI scripts. These CGI programs can be a Python Script, PERL Script, Shell Script, C or C++ program, etc.

CGI Architecture Diagram

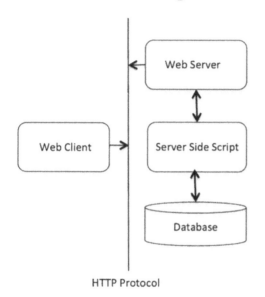

Web Server Support and Configuration

Before you proceed with CGI Programming, make sure that your Web Server supports CGI and it is configured to handle CGI Programs. All the CGI Programs to be executed by the HTTP server are kept in a pre-configured directory. This directory is called CGI Directory and by convention it is named as /var/www/cgi-bin. By convention, CGI files have extension as. cgi, but you can keep your files with python extension .py as well.

By default, the Linux server is configured to run only the scripts in the cgi-bin directory in /var/www. If you want to specify any other directory to run your CGI scripts, comment the following lines in the httpd.conf file –

```
<Directory "/var/www/cgi-bin">

   AllowOverride None

   Options ExecCGI

   Order allow,deny

   Allow from all

</Directory>


<Directory "/var/www/cgi-bin">

Options All

</Directory>
```

Here, we assume that you have Web Server up and running successfully and you are able to run any other CGI program like Perl or Shell, etc.

First CGI Program

Here is a simple link, which is linked to a CGI script called hello.py. This file is kept in /var/www/cgi-bin directory and it has following content. Before running your CGI program, make sure you have change mode of file using chmod 755 hello.py UNIX command to make file executable.

```
#!/usr/bin/python

print "Content-type:text/html\r\n\r\n"

print '<html>'

print '<head>'

print '<title>Hello Word - First CGI Program</title>'

print '</head>'

print '<body>'

print '<h2>Hello Word! This is my first CGI program</h2>'

print '</body>'

print '</html>'
```

If you click hello.py, then this produces the following output –

Hello Word! This is my first CGI program

This hello.py script is a simple Python script, which writes its output on STDOUT file, i.e., screen. There is one important and extra feature available which is first line to be printed Content-type:text/html\r\n\r\n. This line is sent back to the browser and it specifies the content type to be displayed on the browser screen.

By now you must have understood basic concept of CGI and you can write many complicated CGI programs using Python. This script can interact with any other external system also to exchange information such as RDBMS.

HTTP Header

The line Content-type:text/html\r\n\r\n is part of HTTP header which is sent to the browser to understand the content. All the HTTP header will be in the following form –

HTTP Field Name: Field Content

For Example

Content-type: text/html\r\n\r\n

There are few other important HTTP headers, which you will use frequently in your CGI Programming.

Sr.No.	Header & Description
1	**Content-type:** A MIME string defining the format of the file being returned. Example is Content-type:text/html
2	**Expires: Date** The date the information becomes invalid. It is used by the browser to decide when a page needs

to be refreshed. A valid date string is in the format 01 Jan 1998 12:00:00 GMT.

3   **Location: URL**

The URL that is returned instead of the URL requested. You can use this field to redirect a request to any file.

4   **Last-modified: Date**

The date of last modification of the resource.

5   **Content-length: N**

The length, in bytes, of the data being returned. The browser uses this value to report the estimated download time for a file.

6   **Set-Cookie: String**

Set the cookie passed through the *string*

CGI Environment Variables

All the CGI programs have access to the following environment variables. These variables play an important role while writing any CGI program.

Sr.No.   **Variable Name & Description**

1   **CONTENT_TYPE**

    The data type of the content. Used when the client is sending attached content to the server. For example, file upload.

2   **CONTENT_LENGTH**

    The length of the query information. It is available only for POST requests.

3   **HTTP_COOKIE**

    Returns the set cookies in the form of key & value pair.

4   **HTTP_USER_AGENT**

    The User-Agent request-header field contains information about the user agent originating the request. It is name of the web browser.

5   **PATH_INFO**

    The path for the CGI script.

6   **QUERY_STRING**

    The URL-encoded information that is sent with GET method request.

7   **REMOTE_ADDR**

The IP address of the remote host making the request. This is useful logging or for authentication.

8   **REMOTE_HOST**

The fully qualified name of the host making the request. If this information is not available, then REMOTE_ADDR can be used to get IR address.

9   **REQUEST_METHOD**

The method used to make the request. The most common methods are GET and POST.

10   **SCRIPT_FILENAME**

The full path to the CGI script.

11   **SCRIPT_NAME**

The name of the CGI script.

12   **SERVER_NAME**

The server's hostname or IP Address

13   **SERVER_SOFTWARE**

The name and version of the software the server is running.

The name and version of the software the server is running.

Here is small CGI program to list out all the CGI variables.

```
#!/usr/bin/python


import os


print "Content-type: text/html\r\n\r\n";

print "<font size=+1>Environment</font><\br>";

for param in os.environ.keys():

   print "<b>%20s</b>: %s<\br>" % (param,
os.environ[param])
```

GET and POST Methods

You must have come across many situations when you need to pass some information from your browser to web server and ultimately to your CGI Program. Most frequently, browser uses two methods two pass this information to web server. These methods are GET Method and POST Method.

Passing Information using GET method

The GET method sends the encoded user information appended to the page request. The page and the encoded information are separated by the ? character as follows –

```
http://www.test.com/cgi-
bin/hello.py?key1=value1&key2=value2
```

The GET method is the default method to pass
information from browser to web server and it produces
a long string that appears in your browser's
Location:box. Never use GET method if you have
password or other sensitive information to pass to the
server. The GET method has size limitation: only 1024
characters can be sent in a request string. The GET
method sends information using QUERY_STRING
header and will be accessible in your CGI Program
through QUERY_STRING environment variable.

You can pass information by simply concatenating key
and value pairs along with any URL or you can use
HTML <FORM> tags to pass information using GET
method.

Simple URL Example:Get Method

Here is a simple URL, which passes two values to
hello_get.py program using GET method.

```
/cgi-
bin/hello_get.py?first_name=ZARA&last_name=ALI
```

Below is hello_get.py script to handle input given by web
browser. We are going to use cgi module, which makes
it very easy to access passed information –

```
#!/usr/bin/python

# Import modules for CGI handling

import cgi, cgitb
```

```
# Create instance of FieldStorage

form = cgi.FieldStorage()


# Get data from fields

first_name = form.getvalue('first_name')

last_name  = form.getvalue('last_name')


print "Content-type:text/html\r\n\r\n"

print "<html>"

print "<head>"

print "<title>Hello - Second CGI Program</title>"

print "</head>"

print "<body>"
```

This would generate the following result –

Hello ZARA ALI

Simple FORM Example: GET Method

This example passes two values using HTML FORM and submit button. We use same CGI script hello_get.py to handle this input.

```
<form action = "/cgi-bin/hello_get.py" method = "get">
```

```
First Name: <input type = "text" name = "first_name">  <br
/>
```

```
Last Name: <input type = "text" name = "last_name" />
```

```
<input type = "submit" value = "Submit" />
```

```
</form>
```

Here is the actual output of the above form, you enter First and Last Name and then click submit button to see the result.

First
Last Name: |_____| Submit

Name: |_____|

Passing Information Using POST Method

A generally more reliable method of passing information to a CGI program is the POST method. This packages the information in exactly the same way as GET methods, but instead of sending it as a text string after a ? in the URL it sends it as a separate message. This message comes into the CGI script in the form of the standard input.

Below is same hello_get.py script which handles GET as well as POST method.

```
#!/usr/bin/python


# Import modules for CGI handling

import cgi, cgitb
```

```
# Create instance of FieldStorage

form = cgi.FieldStorage()


# Get data from fields

first_name = form.getvalue('first_name')

last_name  = form.getvalue('last_name')


print "Content-type:text/html\r\n\r\n"

print "<html>"

print "<head>"

print "<title>Hello - Second CGI Program</title>"

print "</head>"

print "<body>"

print "<h2>Hello %s %s</h2>" % (first_name, last_name)

print "</body>"

print "</html>"
```

Let us take again same example as above which passes two values using HTML FORM and submit button. We use same CGI script hello_get.py to handle this input.

```
<form action = "/cgi-bin/hello_get.py" method = "post">

First Name: <input type = "text" name = "first_name"><br />

Last Name: <input type = "text" name = "last_name" />
```

```
<input type = "submit" value = "Submit" />

</form>
```

Here is the actual output of the above form. You enter First and Last Name and then click submit button to see the result.

First   Name:

Last Name: Submit

Passing Checkbox Data to CGI Program

Checkboxes are used when more than one option is required to be selected.

Here is example HTML code for a form with two checkboxes –

```
<form action = "/cgi-bin/checkbox.cgi" method = "POST"
target = "_blank">

<input type = "checkbox" name = "maths" value = "on" />
Maths

<input type = "checkbox" name = "physics" value = "on" />
Physics

<input type = "submit" value = "Select Subject" />

</form>
```

The result of this code is the following form –

Maths   Physics   Select Subject

Below is checkbox.cgi script to handle input given by web browser for checkbox button.

```python
#!/usr/bin/python


# Import modules for CGI handling
import cgi, cgitb


# Create instance of FieldStorage
form = cgi.FieldStorage()


# Get data from fields
if form.getvalue('maths'):
    math_flag = "ON"
else:
    math_flag = "OFF"


if form.getvalue('physics'):
    physics_flag = "ON"
else:
    physics_flag = "OFF"


print "Content-type:text/html\r\n\r\n"
```

```
print "<html>"

print "<head>"

print "<title>Checkbox - Third CGI Program</title>"

print "</head>"

print "<body>"

print "<h2> CheckBox Maths is : %s</h2>" % math_flag

print "<h2> CheckBox Physics is : %s</h2>" % physics_flag

print "</body>"

print "</html>"
```

Passing Radio Button Data to CGI Program

Radio Buttons are used when only one option is required to be selected.

Here is example HTML code for a form with two radio buttons –

```
<form action = "/cgi-bin/radiobutton.py" method = "post"
target = "_blank">

<input type = "radio" name = "subject" value = "maths" />
Maths

<input type = "radio" name = "subject" value = "physics" />
Physics

<input type = "submit" value = "Select Subject" />

</form>
```

The result of this code is the following form –

Maths   Physics   Select Subject

Below is radiobutton.py script to handle input given by web browser for radio button –

```
#!/usr/bin/python


# Import modules for CGI handling

import cgi, cgitb


# Create instance of FieldStorage

form = cgi.FieldStorage()


# Get data from fields

if form.getvalue('subject'):

    subject = form.getvalue('subject')

else:

    subject = "Not set"


print "Content-type:text/html\r\n\r\n"

print "<html>"

print "<head>"
```

```
print "<title>Radio - Fourth CGI Program</title>"

print "</head>"

print "<body>"

print "<h2> Selected Subject is %s</h2>" % subject

print "</body>"

print "</html>"
```

Passing Text Area Data to CGI Program

TEXTAREA element is used when multiline text has to be passed to the CGI Program.

Here is example HTML code for a form with a TEXTAREA box –

```
<form action = "/cgi-bin/textarea.py" method = "post" target = "_blank">

<textarea name = "textcontent" cols = "40" rows = "4">

Type your text here...

</textarea>

<input type = "submit" value = "Submit" />

</form>
```

The result of this code is the following form –

Below is textarea.cgi script to handle input given by web browser –

```
#!/usr/bin/python

# Import modules for CGI handling
import cgi, cgitb

# Create instance of FieldStorage
form = cgi.FieldStorage()

# Get data from fields
if form.getvalue('textcontent'):
   text_content = form.getvalue('textcontent')
else:
   text_content = "Not entered"

print "Content-type:text/html\r\n\r\n"
print "<html>"
print "<head>";
print "<title>Text Area - Fifth CGI Program</title>"
print "</head>"
print "<body>"
```

```
print   "<h2>   Entered   Text   Content   is   %s</h2>"   %
text_content

print "</body>"
```

Passing Drop Down Box Data to CGI Program

Drop Down Box is used when we have many options available but only one or two will be selected.

Here is example HTML code for a form with one drop down box –

```
<form  action  =  "/cgi-bin/dropdown.py"  method  =  "post"
target = "_blank">

<select name = "dropdown">

<option value = "Maths" selected>Maths</option>

<option value = "Physics">Physics</option>

</select>

<input type = "submit" value = "Submit"/>

</form>
```

The result of this code is the following form –

Below is dropdown.py script to handle input given by web browser.

```python
#!/usr/bin/python

# Import modules for CGI handling
import cgi, cgitb

# Create instance of FieldStorage
form = cgi.FieldStorage()

# Get data from fields
if form.getvalue('dropdown'):
    subject = form.getvalue('dropdown')
else:
    subject = "Not entered"

print "Content-type:text/html\r\n\r\n"
print "<html>"
print "<head>"
print "<title>Dropdown Box - Sixth CGI Program</title>"
print "</head>"
print "<body>"
print "<h2> Selected Subject is %s</h2>" % subject
```

```
print "</body>"

print "</html>"
```

Using Cookies in CGI

HTTP protocol is a stateless protocol. For a commercial website, it is required to maintain session information among different pages. For example, one user registration ends after completing many pages. How to maintain user's session information across all the web pages?

In many situations, using cookies is the most efficient method of remembering and tracking preferences, purchases, commissions, and other information required for better visitor experience or site statistics.

How It Works?

Your server sends some data to the visitor's browser in the form of a cookie. The browser may accept the cookie. If it does, it is stored as a plain text record on the visitor's hard drive. Now, when the visitor arrives at another page on your site, the cookie is available for retrieval. Once retrieved, your server knows/remembers what was stored.

Cookies are a plain text data record of 5 variable-length fields –

- Expires – The date the cookie will expire. If this is blank, the cookie will expire when the visitor quits the browser.

- Domain – The domain name of your site.

- Path – The path to the directory or web page that sets the cookie. This may be blank if you want to retrieve the cookie from any directory or page.

- Secure – If this field contains the word "secure", then the cookie may only be retrieved with a secure server. If this field is blank, no such restriction exists.

- Name=Value – Cookies are set and retrieved in the form of key and value pairs.

Setting up Cookies

It is very easy to send cookies to browser. These cookies are sent along with HTTP Header before to Content-type field. Assuming you want to set UserID and Password as cookies. Setting the cookies is done as follows –

```
#!/usr/bin/python


print "Set-Cookie:UserID = XYZ;\r\n"

print "Set-Cookie:Password = XYZ123;\r\n"

print "Set-Cookie:Expires = Tuesday, 31-Dec-2007 23:12:40 GMT";\r\n"

print "Set-Cookie:Domain = www.tutorialspoint.com;\r\n"

print "Set-Cookie:Path = /perl;\n"

print "Content-type:text/html\r\n\r\n"

..........Rest of the HTML Content....
```

From this example, you must have understood how to set cookies. We use Set-Cookie HTTP header to set cookies.

It is optional to set cookies attributes like Expires, Domain, and Path. It is notable that cookies are set before sending magic line "Content-

type:text/html\r\n\r\n.

Retrieving Cookies

It is very easy to retrieve all the set cookies. Cookies are stored in CGI environment variable HTTP_COOKIE and they will have following form –

key1 = value1;key2 = value2;key3 = value3....

Here is an example of how to retrieve cookies.

```python
#!/usr/bin/python


# Import modules for CGI handling

from os import environ

import cgi, cgitb


if environ.has_key('HTTP_COOKIE'):

    for cookie in map(strip, split(environ['HTTP_COOKIE'], ';')):

        (key, value ) = split(cookie, '=');

        if key == "UserID":

            user_id = value


        if key == "Password":
```

```
    password = value
```

```
print "User ID  = %s" % user_id

print "Password = %s" % password
```

This produces the following result for the cookies set by above script –

```
User ID = XYZ

Password = XYZ123
```


File Upload Example

To upload a file, the HTML form must have the enctype attribute set to multipart/form-data. The input tag with the file type creates a "Browse" button.

```html
<html>

<body>

   <form enctype = "multipart/form-data"

                 action = "save_file.py" method = "post">

   <p>File: <input type = "file" name = "filename" /></p>

   <p><input type = "submit" value = "Upload" /></p>

   </form>

</body>

</html>
```

The result of this code is the following form –

File:

Upload

Above example has been disabled intentionally to save people uploading file on our server, but you can try above code with your server.

Here is the script save_file.py to handle file upload –

```python
#!/usr/bin/python

import cgi, os

import cgitb; cgitb.enable()


form = cgi.FieldStorage()


# Get filename here.

fileitem = form['filename']


# Test if the file was uploaded

if fileitem.filename:

    # strip leading path from file name to avoid

    # directory traversal attacks

    fn = os.path.basename(fileitem.filename)
```

```
open('/tmp/' + fn, 'wb').write(fileitem.file.read())


  message = 'The file "' + fn + '" was uploaded successfully'

else:

  message = 'No file was uploaded'


print """\

Content-Type: text/html\n

<html>

<body>

  <p>%s</p>

</body>

</html>

""" % (message,)
```

If you run the above script on Unix/Linux, then you need to take care of replacing file separator as follows, otherwise on your windows machine above open() statement should work fine.

```
fn = os.path.basename(fileitem.filename.replace("\\", "/" ))
```

How To Raise a "File Download" Dialog Box?

Sometimes, it is desired that you want to give option where a user can click a link and it will pop up a "File Download" dialogue box to the user instead of displaying actual content. This is very easy and can be achieved through HTTP header. This HTTP header is be different from the header mentioned in previous section.

For example, if you want make a FileName file downloadable from a given link, then its syntax is as follows –

```
#!/usr/bin/python


# HTTP Header

print "Content-Type:application/octet-stream; name = \"FileName\"\r\n";

print "Content-Disposition: attachment; filename = \"FileName\"\r\n\n";


# Actual File Content will go here.

fo = open("foo.txt", "rb")


str = fo.read();

print str


# Close opend file

fo.close()
```

PYTHON - MYSQL DATABASE ACCESS

The Python standard for database interfaces is the Python DB-API. Most Python database interfaces adhere to this standard.

You can choose the right database for your application. Python Database API supports a wide range of database servers such as –

- GadFly
- mSQL
- MySQL
- PostgreSQL
- Microsoft SQL Server 2000
- Informix
- Interbase
- Oracle
- Sybase

Here is the list of available Python database interfaces: Python Database Interfaces and APIs. You must download a separate DB API module for each database you need to access. For example, if you need to access an Oracle database as well as a MySQL database, you must download both the Oracle and the MySQL database modules.

The DB API provides a minimal standard for working with databases using Python structures and syntax wherever possible. This API includes the following –

- Importing the API module.

- Acquiring a connection with the database.

- Issuing SQL statements and stored procedures.

- Closing the connection

We would learn all the concepts using MySQL, so let us talk about MySQLdb module.

What is MySQLdb?

MySQLdb is an interface for connecting to a MySQL database server from Python. It implements the Python Database API v2.0 and is built on top of the MySQL C API.

How do I Install MySQLdb?

Before proceeding, you make sure you have MySQLdb installed on your machine. Just type the following in your Python script and execute it –

```
#!/usr/bin/python
```

```
import MySQLdb
```

If it produces the following result, then it means MySQLdb module is not installed –

```
Traceback (most recent call last):
  File "test.py", line 3, in <module>
    import MySQLdb
ImportError: No module named MySQLdb
```

To install MySQLdb module, use the following command –

For Ubuntu, use the following command -

$ sudo apt-get install python-pip python-dev libmysqlclient-dev

For Fedora, use the following command -

$ sudo dnf install python python-devel mysql-devel redhat-rpm-config gcc

For Python command prompt, use the following command -

pip install

Note – Make sure you have root privilege to install above module.

Database Connection

Before connecting to a MySQL database, make sure of the followings –

- You have created a database TESTDB.

- You have created a table EMPLOYEE in TESTDB.

- This table has fields FIRST_NAME, LAST_NAME, AGE, SEX and INCOME.

- User ID "testuser" and password "test123" are set to access TESTDB.

- Python module MySQLdb is installed properly on your machine.

- You have gone through MySQL tutorial to understand MySQL Basics.

Example

Following is the example of connecting with MySQL database "TESTDB"

```
#!/usr/bin/python

import MySQLdb

# Open database connection
db                                                    =
MySQLdb.connect("localhost","testuser","test123","TESTDB"
)

# prepare a cursor object using cursor() method
cursor = db.cursor()

# execute SQL query using execute() method.
cursor.execute("SELECT VERSION()")

# Fetch a single row using fetchone() method.
data = cursor.fetchone()
print "Database version : %s " % data

# disconnect from server
```

```
db.close()
```

While running this script, it is producing the following result in my Linux machine.

Database version : 5.0.45

If a connection is established with the datasource, then a Connection Object is returned and saved into db for further use, otherwise db is set to None. Next, db object is used to create a cursor object, which in turn is used to execute SQL queries. Finally, before coming out, it ensures that database connection is closed and resources are released.

Creating Database Table

Once a database connection is established, we are ready to create tables or records into the database tables using execute method of the created cursor.

Example

Let us create Database table EMPLOYEE –

```
#!/usr/bin/python


import MySQLdb


# Open database connection

db                                            =
MySQLdb.connect("localhost","testuser","test123","TESTDB"
)
```

```
# prepare a cursor object using cursor() method

cursor = db.cursor()

# Drop table if it already exist using execute() method.

cursor.execute("DROP TABLE IF EXISTS EMPLOYEE")

# Create table as per requirement

sql = """CREATE TABLE EMPLOYEE (

      FIRST_NAME  CHAR(20) NOT NULL,

      LAST_NAME  CHAR(20),

      AGE INT,

      SEX CHAR(1),

      INCOME FLOAT )"""

cursor.execute(sql)

# disconnect from server

db.close()
```

INSERT Operation

It is required when you want to create your records into a database table.

Example

The following example, executes SQL INSERT statement to create a record into EMPLOYEE table –

```python
#!/usr/bin/python

import MySQLdb

# Open database connection
db = MySQLdb.connect("localhost","testuser","test123","TESTDB")

# prepare a cursor object using cursor() method
cursor = db.cursor()

# Prepare SQL query to INSERT a record into the database.
sql = """INSERT INTO EMPLOYEE(FIRST_NAME,
     LAST_NAME, AGE, SEX, INCOME)
     VALUES ('Mac', 'Mohan', 20, 'M', 2000)"""
try:
   # Execute the SQL command
   cursor.execute(sql)
   # Commit your changes in the database
   db.commit()
except:
```

```
# Rollback in case there is any error

db.rollback()


# disconnect from server

db.close()
```

Above example can be written as follows to create SQL queries dynamically –

```
#!/usr/bin/python


import MySQLdb


# Open database connection
db                                                      =
MySQLdb.connect("localhost","testuser","test123","TESTDB"
)


# prepare a cursor object using cursor() method

cursor = db.cursor()


# Prepare SQL query to INSERT a record into the database.

sql = "INSERT INTO EMPLOYEE(FIRST_NAME, \

    LAST_NAME, AGE, SEX, INCOME) \
```

```
    VALUES ('%s', '%s', '%d', '%c', '%d' )" % \

    ('Mac', 'Mohan', 20, 'M', 2000)
try:
    # Execute the SQL command
    cursor.execute(sql)
    # Commit your changes in the database
    db.commit()
except:
    # Rollback in case there is any error
    db.rollback()


# disconnect from server
db.close()
```

Example

Following code segment is another form of execution where you can pass parameters directly –

```
user_id = "test123"
password = "password"


con.execute('insert into Login values("%s", "%s")' % \
        (user_id, password))
```

READ Operation

READ Operation on any database means to fetch some useful information from the database.

Once our database connection is established, you are ready to make a query into this database. You can use either fetchone() method to fetch single record or fetchall() method to fetech multiple values from a database table.

- fetchone() – It fetches the next row of a query result set. A result set is an object that is returned when a cursor object is used to query a table.

- fetchall() – It fetches all the rows in a result set. If some rows have already been extracted from the result set, then it retrieves the remaining rows from the result set.

- rowcount – This is a read-only attribute and returns the number of rows that were affected by an execute() method.

Example

The following procedure queries all the records from EMPLOYEE table having salary more than 1000 –

```
#!/usr/bin/python


import MySQLdb


# Open database connection

db                                    =
MySQLdb.connect("localhost","testuser","test123","TESTDB")
```

```python
# prepare a cursor object using cursor() method
cursor = db.cursor()

sql = "SELECT * FROM EMPLOYEE \
    WHERE INCOME > '%d'" % (1000)
try:
    # Execute the SQL command
    cursor.execute(sql)
    # Fetch all the rows in a list of lists.
    results = cursor.fetchall()
    for row in results:
        fname = row[0]
        lname = row[1]
        age = row[2]
        sex = row[3]
        income = row[4]
        # Now print fetched result
        print "fname=%s,lname=%s,age=%d,sex=%s,income=%d" % \
            (fname, lname, age, sex, income )
except:
```

```
   print "Error: unable to fecth data"


# disconnect from server

db.close()
```

This will produce the following result –

```
fname=Mac, lname=Mohan, age=20, sex=M, income=2000
```

Update Operation

UPDATE Operation on any database means to update one or more records, which are already available in the database.

The following procedure updates all the records having SEX as 'M'. Here, we increase AGE of all the males by one year.

Example

```
#!/usr/bin/python


import MySQLdb


# Open database connection
db                                                    =
MySQLdb.connect("localhost","testuser","test123","TESTDB"
)
```

```
# prepare a cursor object using cursor() method

cursor = db.cursor()


# Prepare SQL query to UPDATE required records

sql = "UPDATE EMPLOYEE SET AGE = AGE + 1
                  WHERE SEX = '%c'" % ('M')
try:
    # Execute the SQL command
    cursor.execute(sql)
    # Commit your changes in the database
    db.commit()
except:
    # Rollback in case there is any error
    db.rollback()


# disconnect from server
db.close()
```

DELETE Operation

DELETE operation is required when you want to delete some records from your database. Following is the procedure to delete all the records from EMPLOYEE where AGE is more than 20 −

Example

```
#!/usr/bin/python

import MySQLdb

# Open database connection
db = MySQLdb.connect("localhost","testuser","test123","TESTDB")

# prepare a cursor object using cursor() method
cursor = db.cursor()

# Prepare SQL query to DELETE required records
sql = "DELETE FROM EMPLOYEE WHERE AGE > '%d'" % (20)
try:
   # Execute the SQL command
   cursor.execute(sql)
   # Commit your changes in the database
   db.commit()
```

```
except:

  # Rollback in case there is any error

  db.rollback()


# disconnect from server

db.close()
```

Performing Transactions

Transactions are a mechanism that ensures data consistency. Transactions have the following four properties –

- Atomicity – Either a transaction completes or nothing happens at all.

- Consistency – A transaction must start in a consistent state and leave the system in a consistent state.

- Isolation – Intermediate results of a transaction are not visible outside the current transaction.

- Durability – Once a transaction was committed, the effects are persistent, even after a system failure.

The Python DB API 2.0 provides two methods to either commit or rollback a transaction.

Example

You already know how to implement transactions. Here is again similar example –

```
# Prepare SQL query to DELETE required records

sql = "DELETE FROM EMPLOYEE WHERE AGE > '%d'" % (20)

try:

    # Execute the SQL command

    cursor.execute(sql)

    # Commit your changes in the database

    db.commit()

except:

    # Rollback in case there is any error

    db.rollback()
```

COMMIT Operation

Commit is the operation, which gives a green signal to database to finalize the changes, and after this operation, no change can be reverted back.

Here is a simple example to call commit method.

```
db.commit()
```

ROLLBACK Operation

If you are not satisfied with one or more of the changes and you want to revert back those changes completely, then use rollback() method.

Here is a simple example to call rollback() method.

```
db.commit()
```

Disconnecting Database

To disconnect Database connection, use close() method.

```
db.close()
```

If the connection to a database is closed by the user with the close() method, any outstanding transactions are rolled back by the DB. However, instead of depending on any of DB lower level implementation details, your application would be better off calling commit or rollback explicitly.

Handling Errors

There are many sources of errors. A few examples are a syntax error in an executed SQL statement, a connection failure, or calling the fetch method for an already canceled or finished statement handle.

The DB API defines a number of errors that must exist in each database module. The following table lists these exceptions.

Sr.No.	Exception & Description

1   **Warning**

Used for non-fatal issues. Must subclass StandardError.

2   **Error**

Base class for errors. Must subclass StandardError.

3   **InterfaceError**

Used for errors in the database module, not the database itself. Must subclass Error.

4   **DatabaseError**

Used for errors in the database. Must subclass Error.

5   **DataError**

Subclass of DatabaseError that refers to errors in the data.

6   **OperationalError**

Subclass of DatabaseError that refers to errors such as the loss of a connection to the database. These errors are generally outside of the control of the Python scripter.

7   **IntegrityError**

Subclass of DatabaseError for situations that would damage the relational integrity, such as uniqueness constraints or foreign keys.

8   **InternalError**

Subclass of DatabaseError that refers to errors internal to the database module, such as a cursor no longer being active.

9   **ProgrammingError**

Subclass of DatabaseError that refers to errors such as a bad table name and other things that can safely be blamed on you.

10   **NotSupportedError**

Subclass of DatabaseError that refers to trying to call unsupported functionality.

Your Python scripts should handle these errors, but before using any of the above exceptions, make sure your MySQLdb has support for that exception. You can get more information about them by reading the DB API 2.0 specification.

NETWORK PROGRAMMING

Python provides two levels of access to network services. At a low level, you can access the basic socket support in the underlying operating system, which allows you to implement clients and servers for both connection-oriented and connectionless protocols.

Python also has libraries that provide higher-level access to specific application-level network protocols, such as FTP, HTTP, and so on.

This chapter gives you understanding on most famous concept in Networking - Socket Programming.

What is Sockets?

Sockets are the endpoints of a bidirectional communications channel. Sockets may communicate within a process, between processes on the same machine, or between processes on different continents.

Sockets may be implemented over a number of different channel types: Unix domain sockets, TCP, UDP, and so on. The socket library provides specific classes for handling the common transports as well as a generic interface for handling the rest.

Sockets have their own vocabulary –

Sr.No.	Term & Description

1   **Domain**

The family of protocols that is used as the transport mechanism. These values are constants such as AF_INET, PF_INET, PF_UNIX, PF_X25, and so on.

2   **type**

The type of communications between the two endpoints, typically SOCK_STREAM for connection-oriented protocols and SOCK_DGRAM for connectionless protocols.

3   **protocol**

Typically zero, this may be used to identify a variant of a protocol within a domain and type.

4   **hostname**

The identifier of a network interface –

- A string, which can be a host name, a dotted-quad address, or an IPV6 address in colon (and possibly dot) notation

- A string "<broadcast>", which specifies an INADDR_BROADCAST address.

- A zero-length string, which specifies INADDR_ANY, or

- An Integer, interpreted as a binary address in host byte order.

| 5 | **port** |

Each server listens for clients calling on one or more ports. A port may be a Fixnum port number, a string containing a port number, or the name of a service.

The socket Module

To create a socket, you must use the socket.socket() function available in socket module, which has the general syntax –

```
s = socket.socket (socket_family, socket_type, protocol=0)
```

Here is the description of the parameters –

- socket_family – This is either AF_UNIX or AF_INET, as explained earlier.
- socket_type – This is either SOCK_STREAM or SOCK_DGRAM.
- protocol – This is usually left out, defaulting to 0.

Once you have socket object, then you can use required functions to create your client or server program. Following is the list of functions required –

Server Socket Methods

Sr.No.	Method & Description
1	**s.bind()** This method binds address (hostname, port number pair) to socket.
2	**s.listen()** This method sets up and start TCP listener.
3	**s.accept()** This passively accept TCP client connection, waiting until connection arrives (blocking).

Client Socket Methods

Sr.No.	Method & Description
1	**s.connect()** This method actively initiates TCP server connection.

General Socket Methods

Sr.No.	Method & Description
1	**s.recv()** This method receives TCP message
2	**s.send()** This method transmits TCP message
3	**s.recvfrom()** This method receives UDP message
4	**s.sendto()** This method transmits UDP message
5	**s.close()** This method closes socket
6	**socket.gethostname()** Returns the hostname.

A Simple Server

To write Internet servers, we use the socket function available in socket module to create a socket object. A socket object is then used to call other functions to setup a socket server.

Now call bind(hostname, port) function to specify a port for your service on the given host.

Next, call the accept method of the returned object. This method waits until a client connects to the port you specified, and then returns a connection object that represents the connection to that client.

```python
#!/usr/bin/python          # This is server.py file


import socket              # Import socket module


s = socket.socket()        # Create a socket object
host = socket.gethostname() # Get local machine name
port = 12345               # Reserve a port for your service.
s.bind((host, port))       # Bind to the port


s.listen(5)                # Now wait for client connection.
while True:
    c, addr = s.accept()   # Establish connection with client.
    print 'Got connection from', addr
```

```
c.send('Thank you for connecting')

c.close()              # Close the connection
```

A Simple Client

Let us write a very simple client program which opens a connection to a given port 12345 and given host. This is very simple to create a socket client using Python's socket module function.

The socket.connect(hosname, port) opens a TCP connection to hostnameon the port. Once you have a socket open, you can read from it like any IO object. When done, remember to close it, as you would close a file.

The following code is a very simple client that connects to a given host and port, reads any available data from the socket, and then exits –

```
#!/usr/bin/python        # This is client.py file


import socket             # Import socket module


s = socket.socket()      # Create a socket object
host = socket.gethostname() # Get local machine name
port = 12345             # Reserve a port for your service.


s.connect((host, port))
```

```
print s.recv(1024)

s.close()                    # Close the socket when done
```

Now run this server.py in background and then run above client.py to see the result.

```
# Following would start a server in background.

$ python server.py &


# Once server is started run client as follows:

$ python client.py
```

This would produce following result –

```
Got connection from ('127.0.0.1', 48437)

Thank you for connecting
```

Python Internet modules

A list of some important modules in Python Network/Internet programming.

Protocol	Common function	Port No	Python module
HTTP	Web pages	80	httplib, urllib, xmlrpclib

NNTP	Usenet news	119	nntplib
FTP	File transfers	20	ftplib, urllib
SMTP	Sending email	25	smtplib
POP3	Fetching email	110	poplib
IMAP4	Fetching email	143	imaplib
Telnet	Command lines	23	telnetlib
Gopher	Document transfers	70	gopherlib, urllib

Please check all the libraries mentioned above to work with FTP, SMTP, POP, and IMAP protocols.

MACHINE LEARNING

A COMPLETE STEP BY STEP GUIDE TO UNDERSTAND MACHINE LEARNING AND ARTIFICIAL INTELLIGENCE FOR BEGINNERS

INTRODUCTION

Machine learning is an application of artificial intelligence (AI) that provides systems the ability to automatically learn and improve from experience without being explicitly programmed. Machine learning focuses on the development of computer programs that can access data and use it learn for themselves.

The process of learning begins with observations or data, such as examples, direct experience, or instruction, in order to look for patterns in data and make better decisions in the future based on the examples that we provide. The primary aim is to allow the computers learn automatically without human intervention or assistance and adjust actions accordingly.

Supervised machine learning algorithms can apply what has been learned in the past to new data using labeled examples to predict future events. Starting from the analysis of a known training dataset, the learning algorithm produces an inferred function to make predictions about the output values. The system is able to provide targets for any new input after sufficient training. The learning algorithm can also compare its output with the correct, intended output and find errors in order to modify the model accordingly.

In contrast, unsupervised machine learning algorithms are used when the information used to train is neither classified nor labeled. Unsupervised learning studies how systems can infer a function to describe a hidden structure from unlabeled data. The system doesn't figure out the right output, but it explores the data and can draw inferences from datasets to describe hidden structures from unlabeled data.

Semi-supervised machine learning algorithms fall somewhere in between supervised and unsupervised learning, since they use both labeled and unlabeled data for training – typically a small amount of labeled data and a large amount of unlabeled data. The systems that use this method are able to considerably improve learning accuracy. Usually, semi-supervised learning is chosen when the acquired labeled data requires skilled and relevant resources in order to train it / learn from it. Otherwise, acquiring unlabeled data generally doesn't require additional resources.

Reinforcement machine learning algorithms is a learning method that interacts with its environment by producing actions and discovers errors or rewards. Trial and error search and delayed reward are the most relevant characteristics of reinforcement learning. This method allows machines and software agents to automatically determine the ideal behavior within a specific context in order to maximize its performance. Simple reward feedback is required for the agent to learn which action is best; this is known as the reinforcement signal.

Machine learning enables analysis of massive quantities of data. While it generally delivers faster, more accurate results in order to identify profitable opportunities or dangerous risks, it may also require additional time and resources to train it properly. Combining machine learning with AI and cognitive technologies can make it even more effective in processing large volumes of information.

WHAT IS MACHINE LEARNING?

"Machine Learning is the science of getting computers to learn and act like humans do, and improve their learning over time in autonomous fashion, by feeding those data and information in the form of observations and real-world interactions."

Machine learning (ML) is a category of an algorithm that allows software applications to become more accurate in predicting outcomes without being explicitly programmed. The basic premise of machine learning is to build algorithms that can receive input data and use statistical analysis to predict an output while updating outputs as new data becomes available.

In a very layman manner, Machine Learning (ML) can be explained as automating and improving the learning process of computers based on their experiences without being actually programmed i.e. without any human assistance. The process starts with feeding good quality data and then training our machines (computers) by building machine learning models using the data and different algorithms. The choice of algorithms depends on what type of data do we have and what kind of task we are trying to automate.

Example: Training of students during exam.

While preparing for the exams students don't actually cram the subject but try to learn it with complete understanding. Before the examination, they feed their machine (brain) with a good amount of high-quality data (questions and answers from different books or teachers notes or online video lectures). Actually, they are training their brain with input as well as output i.e. what kind of approach or logic do they have to solve a different kind of questions. Each time they solve practice test papers and find the performance (accuracy /score) by comparing answers with answer key given, Gradually, the performance keeps on increasing, gaining more confidence with the adopted approach. That's how actually models are built, train machine with data (both inputs and outputs are given to model) and when the time comes test on data (with input only) and achieves our model scores by comparing its answer with the actual output which has not been fed while training. Researchers are working with assiduous efforts to improve algorithms, techniques so that these models perform even much better.

What does exactly learning means for a computer?

A computer is said to be learning from Experiences with respect to some class of Tasks, if its performance in a given Task improves with the Experience.

A computer program is said to learn from experience E with respect to some class of tasks T and performance measure P, if its performance at tasks in T, as measured by P, improves with experience E

Example: playing checkers.

E = the experience of playing many games of checkers

T = the task of playing checkers.

P = the probability that the program will win the next game

In general, any machine learning problem can be assigned to one of two broad classifications:

Supervised learning and Unsupervised learning.

How things work in reality:-

Talking about online shopping, there are millions of users with an unlimited range of interests with respect to brands, colors, price range and many more. While online shopping, buyers tend to search for a number of products. Now, searching a product frequently will make buyer's Facebook, web pages, search engine or that online store start recommending or showing offers on that particular product. There is no one sitting over there to code such task for each and every user, this entire task is completely automatic. Here, ML plays its role. Researchers, data scientists, machine learners build models on the machine using good quality and a huge amount of data and now their machine is automatically performing and even improving with more and more experience and time.

Traditionally, the advertisement was only done using newspapers, magazines and radio but now technology has made us smart enough to do Targeted advertisement (online ad system) which is a way more efficient method to target most receptive audience.

Even in health care also, ML is doing a fabulous job. Researchers and scientists have prepared models to train machines for detecting cancer just by looking at slide – cell images. For humans to perform this task it would have taken a lot of time. But now, no more delay, machines predict the chances of having or not having cancer with some accuracy and doctors just have to give an assurance call, that's it. The answer to – how is this possible is very simple -all that is required, is, high computation machine, a large amount of good quality image data, ML model with good algorithms to achieve state-of-the-art results.

Doctors are using ML even to diagnose patients based on different parameters under consideration.

You might have use IMDB ratings, Google Photos where it recognizes faces, Google Lens where the ML image-text recognition model can extract text from the images you feed in, Gmail which categories E-mail as social, promotion, updates or forum using text classification, which is a part of ML.

How ML works?

Gathering past data in any form suitable for processing. The better the quality of data, the more suitable it will be for modeling

Data Processing – Sometimes, the data collected is in the raw form and it needs to be pre-processed.

Example: Some tuples may have missing values for certain attributes, an, in this case, it has to be filled with suitable values in order to perform machine learning or any form of data mining.

Missing values for numerical attributes such as the price of the house may be replaced with the mean value of the attribute whereas missing values for categorical attributes may be replaced with the attribute with the highest mode. This invariably depends on the types of filters we use. If data is in the form of text or images then converting it to numerical form will be required, be it a list or array or matrix. Simply, Data is to be made relevant and consistent. It is to be converted into a format understandable by the machine

Divide the input data into training, cross-validation and test sets. The ratio between the respective sets must be 6:2:2

Building models with suitable algorithms and techniques on the training set.

Testing our conceptualized model with data which was not fed to the model at the time of training and evaluating its performance using metrics such as F1 score, precision and recall.

HISTORY OF MACHINE LEARNING

Machine Learning is a sub-set of artificial intelligence where computer algorithms are used to autonomously learn from data and information. In machine learning computers don't have to be explicitly programmed but can change and improve their algorithms by themselves.

Today, machine learning algorithms enable computers to communicate with humans, autonomously drive cars, write and publish sport match reports, and find terrorist suspects. I firmly believe machine learning will severely impact most industries and the jobs within them, which is why every manager should have at least some grasp of what machine learning is and how it is evolving.

1950 — Alan Turing creates the "Turing Test" to determine if a computer has real intelligence. To pass the test, a computer must be able to fool a human into believing it is also human.

1952 — Arthur Samuel wrote the first computer learning program. The program was the game of checkers, and the IBM +0% computer improved at the game the more it played, studying which moves made up winning strategies and incorporating those moves into its program.

1957 — Frank Rosenblatt designed the first neural network for computers (the perceptron), which simulate the thought processes of the human brain.

1967 — The "nearest neighbor" algorithm was written, allowing computers to begin using very basic pattern recognition. This could be used to map a route for traveling salesmen, starting at a random city but ensuring they visit all cities during a short tour.

1979 — Students at Stanford University invent the "Stanford Cart" which can navigate obstacles in a room on its own.

1981 — Gerald Dejong introduces the concept of Explanation Based Learning (EBL), in which a computer analyses training data and creates a general rule it can follow by discarding unimportant data.

1985 — Terry Sejnowski invents NetTalk, which learns to pronounce words the same way a baby does.

1990s — Work on machine learning shifts from a knowledge-driven approach to a data-driven approach. Scientists begin creating programs for computers to analyze large amounts of data and draw conclusions — or "learn" — from the results.

1997 — IBM's Deep Blue beats the world champion at chess.

2006 — Geoffrey Hinton coins the term "deep learning" to explain new algorithms that let computers "see" and distinguish objects and text in images and videos.

2010 — The Microsoft MSFT +0% Kinect can track 20 human features at a rate of 30 times per second, allowing people to interact with the computer via movements and gestures.

2011 — IBM's Watson beats its human competitors at Jeopardy.

2011 — Google GOOGL +0% Brain is developed, and its deep neural network can learn to discover and categorize objects much the way a cat does.

2012 – Google's X Lab develops a machine learning algorithm that is able to autonomously browse YouTube videos to identify the videos that contain cats.

2014 – Facebook FB +0% develops DeepFace, a software algorithm that is able to recognize or verify individuals on photos to the same level as humans can.

2015 – Amazon launches its own machine learning platform.

2015 – Microsoft creates the Distributed Machine Learning Toolkit, which enables the efficient distribution of machine learning problems across multiple computers.

2015 – Over 3,000 AI and Robotics researchers, endorsed by Stephen Hawking, Elon Musk and Steve Wozniak (among many others), sign an open letter warning of the danger of autonomous weapons which select and engage targets without human intervention.

2016 – Google's artificial intelligence algorithm beats a professional player at the Chinese board game Go, which is considered the world's most complex board game and is many times harder than chess. The AlphaGo algorithm developed by Google DeepMind managed to win five games out of five in the Go competition.

So are we drawing closer to artificial intelligence? Some scientists believe that's actually the wrong question.

They believe a computer will never "think" in the way that a human brain does, and that comparing the computational analysis and algorithms of a computer to the machinations of the human mind is like comparing apples and oranges.

Regardless, computers' abilities to see, understand, and interact with the world around them is growing at a remarkable rate. And as the quantities of data we produce continue to grow exponentially, so will our computers' ability to process and analyze — and learn from — that data grow and expand.

JARS OF MACHINE LEARNING

The process of getting input and providing output is divided into the following components.

Data

Data is the fuel for Machine learning, Proper history of data on the input and the output is needed to be provided. Example: If an HR manager wants to predict whether or not an employee will leave the company, he needs to provide all the employee information and if they stayed or left.

Task

It specifies what we should do with the given data. It depends on the questions one has to solve with the data available. Example: A task can be to measure the performance of the employee or the happiness level of the employee based on the data.

Model

Based on the input and data we provide, the machine now generates a model or basically a formula which maps input to output.

A model can be like any one of these equations where (x) is input and (y) is the output.

Loss Function

The loss function is the error rate or the difference between the actual output value and the output value predicted by our model. In order to solve a problem, we need to minimize the loss function.

Learning Algorithm

This algorithm is responsible for the minimization of error; it defines a way in which the variables in the equation are given value so the output computed is close to actual output.

Example: In y = mx+c, the values of m and c are found by the learning algorithm so y (computed) is close to y (actual).

Evaluation

In order to find how well our model performs we need to see the accuracy of the model in solving the problem that it was aimed to solve.

Accuracy = Number of correct predictions/Total number of predictions

The accuracy can be found by testing with some parts data which we initially gathered but did not use for training the model.

PROS AND CONS OF MACHINE LEARNING

Machine learning powers many of today's most innovative technologies, from the predictive analytics engines that generate shopping recommendations on Amazon to the artificial intelligence technology used in countless security and antivirus applications worldwide. But like any form of technology, it's not entirely perfect.

Pro: Trends and Patterns Are Identified With Ease

Machine learning is adept at reviewing large volumes of data and identifying patterns and trends that might not be apparent to a human. For instance, a machine learning program may successfully pinpoint a causal relationship between two events. This makes the technology highly effective at data mining, particularly on a continual, ongoing basis, as would be required for an algorithm.

Con: There's a High Level of Error Susceptibility

An error can cause havoc within a machine learning interface, as all events subsequent to the error may be flawed, skewed or just plain undesirable. Errors do occur and it's a susceptibility that developers have thus far been unable to premeditate and negate consistently. These errors can take many forms, which vary according to the way in which you're using machine learning technology. For instance, you might have a faulty sensor that generates a flawed data set. The inaccurate data may then be fed into the machine learning program, which uses it as the basis of an algorithm update. This would cause skewed results in the algorithm's output. In real life, the result could be a situation where related product recommendations are not actually related or similar. So, you might have dog bowls, beach towels and footwear included in the same batch of "related" product recommendations. A computer lacks the ability to understand that these items are not in any way related; this is where human intelligence is required.

Errors are problematic with machine learning due to the autonomous, independent nature of this technology. You run a machine learning program because you don't want a human to babysit the project. However, this means an error may not be discovered immediately. Then, when the problem is identified, it can take a fair amount of time and effort to root out the source of the issue. And finally, you must implement measures to correct the error and remedy any damages that arose from the situation.

Machine learning proponents argue that even with the sometimes time-consuming diagnosis and correction process, this technology is far better than the alternatives when it comes to productivity and efficiency. This stance can be proven in many situations by simply reviewing historical data.

On a related note, machine learning deals in theoretical and statistical truths, which can sometimes differ from literal, real-life truths. It is essential that you account for this fact when using machine learning.

Pro: Machine Learning Improves Over Time

Machine learning technology typically improves efficiency and accuracy over time thanks to the ever-increasing amounts of data that are processed. This gives the algorithm or program more "experience," which can, in turn, be used to make better decisions or predictions.

A great example of this improvement over time involves weather prediction models. Predictions are made by looking at past weather patterns and events; this data is then used to determine what's most likely to occur in a particular scenario. The more data you have in your data set, the greater the accuracy of a given forecast. The same basic concept is also true for algorithms that are used to make decisions or recommendations.

Con: It May Take Time (and Resources) for Machine Learning to Bring Results

Since machine learning occurs over time, as a result of exposure to massive data sets, there may be a period when the algorithm or interface just isn't developed enough for your needs.

In other words, machine learning takes time, especially if you have limited computing power. Handling tremendous volumes of data and running computer models sucks up a lot of computing power, which can potentially be quite costly. So, before turning to machine learning, it's important to consider whether you can invest the amount of time and/or money required to develop the technology to a point where it will be useful. The precise amount of time involved will vary dramatically depending on the data source, the nature of the data and how it's being utilized. Therefore, it's wise to consult with an expert in data mining and machine learning concerning your project.

You should also consider whether you'll need to wait for new data to be generated. For instance, you could have all the computing power on the planet and you will ultimately reach a point where this computing power will do nothing to speed the development of a weather prediction algorithm because there is only so much historical data. You'll simply need to wait as new data is generated—something that can take days, weeks, months or even years.

In a way, this process is similar to the training period required for a new employee. Fortunately, however, a machine learning engine can't walk into your office and put in its two-weeks notice.

Pro: Machine Learning Lets You Adapt Without Human Intervention

Machine learning allows for instantaneous adaptation, without the need for human intervention.

An excellent example of this can be found in security and anti-virus software programs, which leverage machine learning and AI technology to implement filters and other safeguards in response to new threats.

These systems use machine learning to identify new threats and trends. Then, the AI technology is used to implement the appropriate measures for neutralizing or protecting against that threat. Machine learning has eliminated the gap between the time when a new threat is identified and the time when a response is issued. This near-immediate response is critical in a niche where bots, viruses, worms, hackers and other cyber threats can impact thousands or even millions of people in minutes.

Pro and Con: Automation

Machine learning is a key component in technologies such as predictive analytics and artificial intelligence. The automated nature of machine learning means it can save time and money, as developers and analysts are freed up to perform high-level tasks that a computer simply cannot handle.

On the flip side, you have a computer running the show and that's something that is certain to make any developer squirm with discomfort. For now, technology is imperfect. Still, there are workarounds. For instance, if you're employing machine learning technology in order to develop an algorithm, you might program the machine learning interface so it just suggests improvements or changes that must be implemented by a human.

This workaround adds a human gatekeeper to the equation, thereby eliminating the potential for problems that can arise when a computer is in charge. After all, an algorithm update that looks good on paper may not work effectively when it's put into practice. If your system is configured to automatically implement improvements that are suggested by the machine learning interface, operations could run off the rails until a human intervenes, identifies the problem and takes corrective measures.

Like many technologies, machine learning isn't right for every company or every application, and the impact of these pros and cons will vary according to your unique objectives. But there are many businesses that would enjoy a tremendous benefit from machine learning and related technologies like AI and predictive analytics. If you fall into the latter group, SevenTablets can help. Our world-class team of developers specialize in many of the newest technologies, including machine learning, blockchain, predictive analytics, augmented reality, virtual reality, artificial intelligence and natural language processing.

BENEFITS OF MACHINE LEARNING

Simplifies Product Marketing and Assists in Accurate Sales Forecasts

ML helps enterprises in multiple ways to promote their products better and make accurate sales forecasts. ML offers huge advantages to sales and marketing sector, with the major ones being -

Massive Data Consumption from Unlimited Sources

ML virtually consumes unlimited amount of comprehensive data. The consumed data can then be used to constantly review and modify your sales and marketing strategies based on the customer behavioral patterns. Once your model is trained, it will be able to identify highly relevant variables. Consequently, you will be able to get focused data feeds by foregoing long and complicated integrations.

Rapid Analysis Prediction and Processing

The rate at which ML consumes data and identifies relevant data makes it possible for you to take appropriate actions at the right time. For instance, ML will optimize the best subsequent offer for your customer. Consequently, the customer will be able to see the right offer at a given point of time, without you actually investing time to plan and make the right ad visible for your customers.

Interpret Past Customer Behaviors

ML will let you analyze the data related to past behaviors or outcomes and interpret them. Therefore, based on the new and different data you will be able make better predictions of customer behaviors.

Facilitates Accurate Medical Predictions and Diagnoses

In healthcare industry, ML helps in easy identification of high-risk patients, make near perfect diagnoses, recommend best possible medicines, and predict readmissions. These are predominantly based on the available datasets of anonymous patient records as well as the symptoms exhibited by them. Near accurate diagnoses and better medicine recommendations will facilitate faster patient recovery without the need for extraneous medications. In this way, ML makes it possible to improve patient health at minimal costs in the medical sector.

Simplifies Time-Intensive Documentation in Data Entry

Data duplication and inaccuracy are the major issues confronted by organizations wanting to automate their data entry process. Well, this situation can be significantly improved by predictive modeling and machine learning algorithms. With this, machines can perform time-intensive data entry tasks, leaving your skilled resources free to focus on other value-adding duties.

Improves Precision of Financial Rules and Models

ML also has a significant impact on the finance sector. Some of the common machine learning benefits in Finance include portfolio management, algorithmic trading, loan underwriting and most importantly fraud detection. In addition, according to a report on 'The Future of Underwriting' published by Ernst and Young, ML facilitates continual data assessments for detecting and analyzing anomalies and nuances. This helps in improving the precision of financial models and rules.

Easy Spam Detection

Spam detection was one of the earliest problems solved by ML. Few years ago email providers made use of rule-based techniques to filter out spam. However, with the advent of ML, spam filters are making new rules using brain-like neural networks to eliminate spam mails. The neural networks recognize phishing messages and junk mail by evaluating the rules across a huge network of computers.

Increases the Efficiency of Predictive Maintenance in the Manufacturing Industry

Manufacturing firms have corrective as well as preventive maintenance practices in place. However, these are often costly and inefficient. This is exactly where ML can be of great help. ML helps in the creation of highly efficient predictive maintenance plans. Following such predictive maintenance plans will minimize the chances of unexpected failures, thereby reducing unnecessary preventive maintenance activities.

Better Customer Segmentation and Accurate Lifetime Value Prediction

Customer segmentation and lifetime value prediction are the major challenges faced by marketers today. Sales and marketing units will have enormous amounts of relevant data sourced from various channels, such as lead data, website visitors and email campaigns. However, accurate predictions for incentives and individual marketing offers can be easily achieved with ML. Savvy marketers now use ML to eliminate guess work associated with data-driven marketing. For instance, using the data representing the behavioral pattern of a particular set of users during a trial period will help businesses in predicting the probability of conversion to paid version. Such a model triggers customer interventions to better engage the customers in the trial and also persuade customers to convert early.

Recommending the Right Product

Product recommendation is an important aspect of any sales and marketing strategy including upselling and cross-selling. ML models will analyze the purchase history of a customer and based on that they identify those products from your product inventory in which a customer is interested in. The algorithm will identify hidden patterns among the items and will then group similar products into clusters. This process is known as unsupervised learning, which is a specific type of ML algorithm. Such a model will enable businesses to make better product recommendations for their customers, thereby motivating product purchase. In this way, unsupervised learning helps in creating a superior product-based recommendation system.

All these applications make machine learning a top value-producing digital innovation trend. Furthermore, ML enables businesses to effortlessly discover new trends and patterns from large and diverse data sets. Businesses can now automate analysis to interpret business interactions, which were traditionally done by humans, to take evidence-based actions. This empowers enterprises to deliver new, personalized or differentiated products and services. Therefore, considering ML as a strategic initiative can be a lucrative decision. However, deployment might carry certain business risk. Therefore, it is better to approach investment decisions with utmost care.

TYPES OF MACHINE LEARNING

What is Supervised Learning?

Supervised Learning is the one, where you can consider the learning is guided by a teacher. We have a dataset which acts as a teacher and its role is to train the model or the machine. Once the model gets trained it can start making a prediction or decision when new data is given to it.

What is Unsupervised Learning?

The model learns through observation and finds structures in the data. Once the model is given a dataset, it automatically finds patterns and relationships in the dataset by creating clusters in it. What it cannot do is add labels to the cluster, like it cannot say this a group of apples or mangoes, but it will separate all the apples from mangoes.

Suppose we presented images of apples, bananas and mangoes to the model, so what it does, based on some patterns and relationships it creates clusters and divides the dataset into those clusters. Now if a new data is fed to the model, it adds it to one of the created clusters.

What is Reinforcement Learning?

It is the ability of an agent to interact with the environment and find out what is the best outcome. It follows the concept of hit and trial method. The agent is rewarded or penalized with a point for a correct or a wrong answer, and on the basis of the positive reward points gained the model trains itself. And again once trained it gets ready to predict the new data presented to it.

WHY YOU SHOULD LEARN MACHINE LEARNING?

Machine Learning is no longer just a niche subfield of computer science but technology giants have been using it for years. Machine learning products are being used daily, perhaps without realizing it. The future of machine learning is already here, it's just that machine learning career is exploding now because of smart algorithms being used everywhere from email to mobile apps to marketing campaigns. If you are in search of the most in-demand and most-exciting career domains, gearing up yourself with machine learning skills is a good move now.

"Artificial Intelligence, deep learning, machine learning—whatever you're doing if you don't understand it—learn it. Because otherwise you're going to be a dinosaur within 3 years."

1) Learning machine learning brings in better career opportunities

AI driven services were worth $1.9 billion in 2016 and are anticipated to rise to $2.7 billion by end of 2017 of which 23% of the revenue comes through machine learning technology.

Machine learning is the shining star of the moment. With every industry looking to apply AI in their domain, studying machine learning opens world of opportunities to develop cutting edge machine learning applications in various verticals – such as cyber security, image recognition, medicine, or face recognition. With several machine learning companies on the verge of hiring skilled ML engineers, it is becoming the brain behind business intelligence. Netflix announced prize worth $1 million to the first individual who could enhance the accuracy of its recommendation ML algorithm by 10%. This is a clear evidence on how significant even a slight enhancement is in the accuracy of recommendation machine learning algorithms to improve the profitability of Netflix. Every customer- centric organization is looking to adopt machine learning technology and is the next big thing paving opportunities for IT professionals. Machine learning algorithms have become the darlings of business and consumers so if you want to put yourselves somewhere in the upper echelon of software engineers then this is the best time to learn ML.

2) Machine Learning Engineers earn a pretty penny

The cost of a top, world-class machine learning expert can be related to that of a top NFL quarterback prospect. According to SimplyHired.com, the average machine learning engineer salary is $142,000.An experienced machine learning engineer can earn up to $195, 752.

3) Machine Learning Jobs on the rise

"You need a special kind of person to build a hammer, but once you build it, you can give it to many people who will use it to build a house."

The major hiring is happening in all top tech companies in search of those special kind of people (machine learning engineers) who can build a hammer (machine learning algorithms). The job market for machine learning engineers is not just hot but it's sizzling.

According to the popular job portal Indeed, the number of open machine learning jobs have been steadily rising from 2014 to the onset of 2016, from 60 job postings per million to more than 100. The number of job postings jumped up to 150 postings per million by end of 2016. Indeed job trends report also reveals that the number of machine learning engineer job postings outstrip the number of searches for machine learning jobs – 100 million searches vs. 150 job postings.

4) CIO's Lament Lack of Machine Learning Skills

The new victim to the continuing skills gap to plague many sections of the software world is digital transformation with the use of machine learning. According to Gartner report, any CIO looking to hire talent with machine learning skills in New York taps into a talent pool of merely 32 experts, of which only 16 are potential candidates. Any organization faces several challenges to begin with machine learning and one of the top concerns for these companies is shortage of personnel with machine learning skills.

A New York Time report estimates that there are less than 10,000 people in the world that have the required background and skills necessary for AI related jobs (Machine learning and Deep Learning). The demand for skilled machine learning engineers far exceeds that modest number. Spotting these untapped machine learning opportunities does not require a PhD in Math or Statistics but a brief trip back to basics of Math, Algebra and Statistics along with a comprehensive machine learning MOOC is what required to get started for a successful machine learning career.

5) Machine learning is linked directly to Data Science

Machine learning appears as a shadow of data science. Machine learning career endows you with two hats, one is for a machine learning engineer job and the other is for a data scientist job. Becoming competent in both the fields makes an individual a hot commodity to most of the employers. It means that you can analyse tons of data, extract value and glean insight from it, and later make use of that information to train a machine learning model to predict results. In many organizations, a machine learning engineer often partners with a data scientist for better synchronization of work products. Furthermore, data scientist has been voted the Sexiest Job of 21st Century so one can get started as a data scientist specializing in Machine Learning and become more desirable to employers.

MACHINE LEARNING: HOW TO GET STARTED

Gone are the days when ML knowledge used to be an exclusive preserve of Ph.D. researchers and students. Today, you can teach yourself ML without needing to enroll in a University – although a formal education may be quite beneficial. If you aren't cut out for higher degrees, here are some useful tips to get started with ML.

Learn a Programming Language: You NEED to have some programming knowledge under your belt to get started. Python comes in handy, because it's used in many machine learning projects due to its possession of tons of data science libraries. It's also relatively easy to learn and comprehend.

Get a high-end PC: Chances are you'd make use of only small datasets when starting out. But as time passes by, you might want to delve into more complex projects. To get the best of the learning experience, you should ensure that your PC satisfies certain requirements, including possessing a good enough Random Access Memory (RAM) and storage. Also to play with Deep Learning (an ML algorithm), you'd need high-quality Graphical Processing Units (GPUs).

Learn the prerequisites: Machine Learning draws a lot from three areas in Mathematics: Statistics, Linear Algebra and Calculus. If you aren't comfortable with Math, don't fret. Many of the things you actually need to learn in order to get started, are quite basic.

Read ML Academic Papers: Many ML papers are published regularly, and reading tons of them is a good way to learn new things and keep up with the pace of ML research.

Read Blogs and Follow Online Communities: Follow blogs and online communities that can help fast track the learning process. Reddit's machine learning channel is a good example of the latter.

Practice: Practice makes perfect, they say. So, try your hands at machine learning projects and participate in contests hosted on Kaggle and similar sites.

In conclusion, there's no stopping ML in today's world. If you're look forward to supercharging your career, learning ML might be the way to go

MACHINE LEARNING METHODS

A machine learning algorithm, also called model, is a mathematical expression that represents data in the context of a problem, often a business problem. The aim is to go from data to insight. For example, if an online retailer wants to anticipate sales for the next quarter, they might use a machine learning algorithm that predicts those sales based on past sales and other relevant data. Similarly, a windmill manufacturer might visually monitor important equipment and feed the video data through algorithms trained to identify dangerous cracks.

Word Embeddings

We apply supervised ML techniques when we have a piece of data that we want to predict or explain. We do so by using previous data of inputs and outputs to predict an output based on a new input. For example, you could use supervised ML techniques to help a service business that wants to predict the number of new users who will sign up for the service next month. By contrast, unsupervised ML looks at ways to relate and group data points without the use of a target variable to predict. In other words, it evaluates data in terms of traits and uses the traits to form clusters of items that are similar to one another. For example, you could use unsupervised learning techniques to help a retailer that wants to segment products with similar characteristics — without having to specify in advance which characteristics to use.

Regression

Regression methods fall within the category of supervised ML. They help to predict or explain a particular numerical value based on a set of prior data, for example predicting the price of a property based on previous pricing data for similar properties.

The simplest method is linear regression where we use the mathematical equation of the line (y = m * x + b) to model a data set. We train a linear regression model with many data pairs (x, y) by calculating the position and slope of a line that minimizes the total distance between all of the data points and the line. In other words, we calculate the slope (m) and the y-intercept (b) for a line that best approximates the observations in the data.

Let's consider a more a concrete example of linear regression. I once used a linear regression to predict the energy consumption (in kWh) of certain buildings by gathering together the age of the building, number of stories, square feet and the number of plugged wall equipment. Since there were more than one input (age, square feet, etc...), I used a multi-variable linear regression. The principle was the same as a simple one-to-one linear regression, but in this case the "line" I created occurred in multi-dimensional space based on the number of variables.

Regression techniques run the gamut from simple (like linear regression) to complex (like regularized linear regression, polynomial regression, decision trees and random forest regressions, neural nets, among others). But don't get bogged down: start by studying simple linear regression, master the techniques, and move on from there.

Classification

Another class of supervised ML, classification methods predict or explain a class value. For example, they can help predict whether or not an online customer will buy a product. The output can be yes or no: buyer or not buyer. But classification methods aren't limited to two classes. For example, a classification method could help to assess whether a given image contains a car or a truck. In this case, the output will be 3 different values: 1) the image contains a car, 2) the image contains a truck, or 3) the image contains neither a car nor a truck.

The simplest classification algorithm is logistic regression — which makes it sounds like a regression method, but it's not. Logistic regression estimates the probability of an occurrence of an event based on one or more inputs.

For instance, a logistic regression can take as inputs two exam scores for a student in order to estimate the probability that the student will get admitted to a particular college. Because the estimate is a probability, the output is a number between 0 and 1, where 1 represents complete certainty. For the student, if the estimated probability is greater than 0.5, then we predict that he or she will be admitted. If the estimated probabiliy is less than 0.5, we predict the he or she will be refused.

Clustering

With clustering methods, we get into the category of unsupervised ML because their goal is to group or cluster observations that have similar characteristics. Clustering methods don't use output information for training, but instead let the algorithm define the output.

In clustering methods, we can only use visualizations to inspect the quality of the solution.

The most popular clustering method is K-Means, where "K" represents the number of clusters that the user chooses to create. (Note that there are various techniques for choosing the value of K, such as the elbow method.)

Roughly, what K-Means does with the data points:

Randomly chooses K centers within the data.

Assigns each data point to the closest of the randomly created centers.

Re-computes the center of each cluster.

If centers don't change (or change very little), the process is finished. Otherwise, we return to step 2. (To prevent ending up in an infinite loop if the centers continue to change, set a maximum number of iterations in advance.)

The next plot applies K-Means to a data set of buildings. Each column in the plot indicates the efficiency for each building. The four measurements are related to air conditioning, plugged-in equipment (microwaves, refrigerators, etc...), domestic gas, and heating gas. We chose K=2 for clustering, which makes it easy to interpret one of the clusters as the group of efficient buildings and the other cluster as the group of inefficient buildings. To the left you see the location of the buildings and to right you see two of the four dimensions we used as inputs: plugged-in equipment and heating gas.

Dimensionality Reduction

As the name suggests, we use dimensionality reduction to remove the least important information (sometime redundant columns) from a data set. In practice, data sets are with hundreds or even thousands of columns (also called features), so reducing the total number is vital. For instance, images can include thousands of pixels, not all of which matter to your analysis. Or when testing microchips within the manufacturing process, you might have thousands of measurements and tests applied to every chip, many of which provide redundant information. In these cases, you need dimensionality reduction algorithms to make the data set manageable.

The most popular dimensionality reduction method is Principal Component Analysis (PCA), which reduces the dimension of the feature space by finding new vectors that maximize the linear variation of the data. PCA can reduce the dimension of the data dramatically and without losing too much information when the linear correlations of the data are strong. (And in fact you can also measure the actual extent of the information loss and adjust accordingly.)

Another popular method is t-Stochastic Neighbor Embedding (t-SNE), which does non-linear dimensionality reduction. People typically use t-SNE for data visualization, but you can also use it for machine learning tasks like reducing the feature space and clustering, to mention just a few.

Ensemble Methods

Imagine you've decided to build a bicycle because you are not feeling happy with the options available in stores and online. You might begin by finding the best of each part you need. Once you assemble all these great parts, the resulting bike will outshine all the other options.

Ensemble methods use this same idea of combining several predictive models (supervised ML) to get higher quality predictions than each of the models could provide on its own. For example, the Random Forest algorithms is an ensemble method that combines many Decision Trees trained with different samples of the data sets. As a result, the quality of the predictions of a Random Forest is higher than the quality of the predictions estimated with a single Decision Tree.

Think of ensemble methods as a way to reduce the variance and bias of a single machine learning model. That's important because any given model may be accurate under certain conditions but inaccurate under other conditions. With another model, the relative accuracy might be reversed. By combining the two models, the quality of the predictions is balanced out.

The great majority of top winners of Kaggle competitions use ensemble methods of some kind. The most popular ensemble algorithms are Random Forest, XGBoost and LightGBM.

Neural Networks and Deep Learning

In contrast to linear and logistic regressions which are considered linear models, the objective of neural networks is to capture non-linear patterns in data by adding layers of parameters to the model. In the image below, the simple neural net has four inputs, a single hidden layer with five parameters, and an output layer.

Neural Network with One Hidden Layer.

In fact, the structure of neural networks is flexible enough to build our well-known linear and logistic regression. The term Deep learning comes from a neural net with many hidden layers and encapsulates a wide variety of architectures.

It's especially difficult to keep up with developments in deep learning, in part because the research and industry communities have doubled down on their deep learning efforts, spawning whole new methodologies every day.

Deep Learning: Neural Network with Many Hidden Layers.

For the best performance, deep learning techniques require a lot of data — and a lot of compute power since the method is self-tuning many parameters within huge architectures. It quickly becomes clear why deep learning practitioners need very powerful computers enhanced with GPUs (graphical processing units).

In particular, deep learning techniques have been extremely successful in the areas of vision (image classification), text, audio and video. The most common software packages for deep learning are Tensorflow and PyTorch.

Transfer Learning

Let's pretend that you're a data scientist working in the retail industry. You've spent months training a high-quality model to classify images as shirts, t-shirts and polos. Your new task is to build a similar model to classify images of dresses as jeans, cargo, casual, and dress pants. Can you transfer the knowledge built into the first model and apply it to the second model? Yes, you can, using Transfer Learning.

Transfer Learning refers to re-using part of a previously trained neural net and adapting it to a new but similar task. Specifically, once you train a neural net using data for a task, you can transfer a fraction of the trained layers and combine them with a few new layers that you can train using the data of the new task. By adding a few layers, the new neural net can learn and adapt quickly to the new task.

The main advantage of transfer learning is that you need less data to train the neural net, which is particularly important because training for deep learning algorithms is expensive in terms of both time and money (computational resources) — and of course it's often very difficult to find enough labeled data for the training.

Assume that for the shirt model you use a neural net with 20 hidden layers. After running a few experiments, you realize that you can transfer 18 of the shirt model layers and combine them with one new layer of parameters to train on the images of pants. The pants model would therefore have 19 hidden layers. The inputs and outputs of the two task are different but the re-usable layers may be summarizing information that is relevant to both, for example aspects of cloth, fasteners, and shape.

Transfer learning has become more and more popular and there are now many solid pre-trained models available for common deep learning tasks like image and text classification.

Reinforcement Learning

Imagine a mouse in a maze trying to find hidden pieces of cheese. The more times we expose the mouse to the maze, the better it gets at finding the cheese. At first, the mouse might move randomly, but after some time, the mouse's experience helps it realize which actions bring it closer to the cheese.

The process for the mouse mirrors what we do with Reinforcement Learning (RL) to train a system or a game. Generally speaking, RL is a machine learning method that helps an agent learn from experience. By recording actions and using a trial-and-error approach in a set environment, RL can maximize a cumulative reward. In our example, the mouse is the agent and the maze is the environment. The set of possible actions for the mouse are: move front, back, left or right. The reward is the cheese.

You can use RL when you have little to no historical data about a problem, because it doesn't need information in advance (unlike traditional machine learning methods). In a RL framework, you learn from the data as you go. Not surprisingly, RL is especially successful with games, especially games of "perfect information" like chess and Go. With games, feedback from the agent and the environment comes quickly, allowing the model to learn fast. The downside of RL is that it can take a very long time to train if the problem is complex.

Natural Language Processing

A huge percentage of the world's data and knowledge is in some form of human language. Can you imagine being able to read and comprehend thousands of books, articles and blogs in seconds? Obviously, computers can't yet fully understand human text but we can train them to do certain tasks. For example, we can train our phones to autocomplete our text messages or to correct misspelled words. We can even teach a machine to have a simple conversation with a human.

Natural Language Processing (NLP) is not a machine learning method per se, but rather a widely used technique to prepare text for machine learning. Think of tons of text documents in a variety of formats (word, online blogs, ….). Most of these text documents will be full of typos, missing characters and other words that needed to be filtered out. At the moment, the most popular package for processing text is NLTK (Natural Language ToolKit), created by researchers at Stanford.

The simplest way to map text into a numerical representation is to compute the frequency of each word within each text document. Think of a matrix of integers where each row represents a text document and each column represents a word. This matrix representation of the word frequencies is commonly called Term Frequency Matrix (TFM). From there, we can create another popular matrix representation of a text document by dividing each entry on the matrix by a weight of how important each word is within the entire corpus of documents. This method is called Term Frequency Inverse Document Frequency (TFIDF) and it typically works better for machine learning tasks.

Word Embeddings

TFM and TFIDF are numerical representations of text documents that only consider frequency and weighted frequencies to represent text documents. By contrast, word embeddings can capture the context of a word in a document. With the word context, embeddings can quantify the similarity between words, which in turn allows us to do arithmetic with words.

Word2Vec is a method based on neural nets that maps words in a corpus to a numerical vector. We can then use these vectors to find synonyms, perform arithmetic operations with words, or to represent text documents (by taking the mean of all the word vectors in a document). For example, let's assume that we use a sufficiently big corpus of text documents to estimate word embeddings. Let's also assume that the words king, queen, man and woman are part of the corpus. Let say that vector('word') is the numerical vector that represents the word 'word'. To estimate vector('woman'), we can perform the arithmetic operation with vectors:

vector('king') + vector('woman') — vector('man') ~ vector('queen')

Arithmetic with Word (Vectors) Embeddings.

Word representations allow finding similarities between words by computing the cosine similarity between the vector representation of two words. The cosine similarity measures the angle between two vectors.

We compute word embeddings using machine learning methods, but that's often a pre-step to applying a machine learning algorithm on top. For instance, suppose we have access to the tweets of several thousand Twitter users. Also suppose that we know which of these Twitter users bought a house. To predict the probability of a new Twitter user buying a house, we can combine Word2Vec with a logistic regression.

TOP MACHINE LEARNING ALGORITHMS

1. Principal Component Analysis (PCA)/SVD

This is one of the basic machine learning algorithms. It allows you to reduce the dimension of the data, losing the least amount of information. It is used in many areas, such as object recognition, computer vision, data compression, etc. The computation of the principal components is reduced to calculating the eigenvectors and eigenvalues of the covariance matrix of the original data or to the singular decomposition of the data matrix.

We can express several signs through one, merge, so to speak, and work already with a simpler model. Of course, most likely, it will not be possible to avoid information loss, but the PCA method will help to minimize it.

2. Least Squares and Polynomial Fitting

The method of least squares is a mathematical method used to solve various problems, based on minimizing the sum of squares of deviations of some functions from the desired variables. It can be used to "solve" overdetermined systems of equations (when the number of equations exceeds the number of unknowns), to search for solutions in the case of ordinary (not overdetermined) nonlinear systems of equations, as well as to approximate the point values of a certain function.

b. Constrained Linear Regression

The least squares method can confuse overshoots, false fields, etc. Restrictions are needed to reduce the variance of the line that we put in the data set. The correct solution is to match the linear regression model, which ensures that the weights do not behave "badly".

Models can be L1 (LASSO) or L2 (Ridge Regression) or both (elastic regression).

3. K-Means Clustering

Everyone's favorite uncontrolled clustering algorithm. But, let's clarify what clustering is:

Clustering (or cluster analysis) is the task of breaking up a set of objects into groups called clusters. Inside each group, there should be "similar" objects, and the objects of different groups should be as different as possible. The main difference between clustering and classification is that the list of groups is not clearly defined and is determined during the operation of the algorithm.

The k-means algorithm is the simplest, but at the same time, rather inaccurate clustering method in the classical implementation. It splits the set of elements of a vector space into a previously known number of clusters k.

The algorithm seeks to minimize the standard deviation at the points of each cluster. The basic idea is that at each iteration the center of mass is recalculated for each cluster obtained in the previous step, then the vectors are divided into clusters again according to which of the new centers was closer in the selected metric. The algorithm terminates when no cluster changes at any iteration.

4. Logistic Regression

Logistic regression is limited to linear regression with non-linearity (sigmoid function or tanh is mainly used) after applying weights, therefore, the output limit is close to + / — classes (which equals 1 and 0 in the case of sigmoid). Cross-entropy loss functions are optimized using the gradient descent method.

Note: logistic regression is used for classification, not regression. In general, it is similar to a single-layer neural network. Learn using optimization techniques such as gradient descent or L-BFGS. NLP developers often use it, calling it "the maximum entropy classification method".

5. Support Vector Machines (SVM)

SVM is a linear model, such as linear/logistic regression. The difference is that it has a margin-based loss function. You can optimize the loss function using optimization methods, for example, L-BFGS or SGD.

One unique thing that SVMs can do is to study classifier classifiers.

SVM can be used to train classifiers (even regressors).

6. Feed-Forward Neural Networks

Basically, these are multi-level logistic regression classifiers. Many layers of scales are separated by non-linearities (sigmoid, tanh, relu + softmax and cool new selu). They are also called multilayer perceptrons. FFNN can be used for classifying and "learning without a teacher" as autoencoders.

FFNN can be used to train a classifier or extract functions as autoencoders.

7. Convolutional Neural Networks

Practically all modern achievements in the field of machine learning were achieved by dint of convolutional neural networks. They are used for image classification, object detection, or even image segmentation. Invented by Jan Lekun at the beginning of the 1990s, networks have convolutional layers that act as hierarchical object extractors. You can use them for working with text (and even for working with graphics).

8. Recurrent Neural Networks (RNNs)

RNNs model sequences by applying the same set of weights recursively to the state of the aggregator at time t and input at time t. Pure RNNs are rarely used now, but its analogs, for example, LSTM and GRU, are the most up-to-date in most sequence modeling problems.

LSTM, which is used instead of a simple dense layer in pure RNN.

Use RNN for any task of text classification, machine translation, language modeling.

9. Conditional Random Fields (CRFs)

They are used to simulate a sequence like an RNN and can be used in conjunction with an RNN. They can also be used in other tasks of structured prediction, for example, in image segmentation. CRF models each element of the sequence (say, a sentence), so that the neighbors affect the label of the component in the sequence, and not all labels that are independent of each other.

Use CRF for sequences of sequences (in text, image, time series, DNA, etc.).

10. Decision Trees

One of the most common machine learning algorithms. Used in statistics and data analysis for predictive models. The structure represents the "leaves" and "branches". Attributes of the objective function depend on the "branches" of the decision tree, the values of the objective function are recorded in the "leaves", and the remaining nodes contain attributes for which the cases differ.

To classify a new case, you need to go down the tree to the leaf and give the appropriate value. The goal is to create a model that predicts the value of the target variable based on several input variables.

STEP GUIDE TO MASTERING MACHINE LEARNING

1. Preprocessing of Data

Each machine learning algorithm works differently, and has different data requirements. For example, some algorithms need numeric features to be normalized, and some require text processing that splits the text into words and phrases, which can be very complicated for languages like Japanese. Users should expect their automated machine learning platform to know how to best prepare data for every algorithm and following best practices for data partitioning.

2. Feature Engineering

Feature engineering is the process of altering the data to help machine learning algorithms work better, which is often time-consuming and can be expensive. While some feature engineering requires domain knowledge of the data and business rules, most feature engineering is generic. A true automated machine learning platform will engineer new features from existing numeric, categorical, and text features. The system should understand which algorithms benefit from extra feature engineering and which don't, and only generate features that make sense given the data characteristics.

3. Diverse Algorithms

Every dataset contains unique information that reflects the individual events and characteristics of a business. Due to the variety of situations and conditions represented in the data, one algorithm cannot successfully solve every possible business problem or dataset. Automated machine learning platforms need access to a diverse repository of algorithms to test against the data in order to find the right algorithm to solve the challenge at hand. And, the platform should be updated continually with the most promising new machine learning algorithms, including those from the open source community.

4. Algorithm Selection

Having access to hundreds of algorithms is great, but many organizations don't have the time to try every algorithm on their data. And some algorithms aren't suited to their data or data sizes, while others are extremely unlikely to work well on their data altogether. An automated machine learning platform should know which algorithms are right for a business' data and test the data on only the appropriate algorithms to achieve results faster.

5. Training and Tuning

It's standard for machine learning software to train an algorithm on the data, but often there is still some hyperparameter tuning required to optimize the algorithm's performance. In addition, it's important to understand which features to leave in or out, and which feature selections work best for different models. An effective automated machine learning platform employs smart hyperparameter tuning for each individual model, as well as automatic feature selection, to improve both the speed and accuracy of a model.

6. Ensembling

Teams of algorithms are called "ensembles" or "blenders," with each algorithm's strengths balancing out the weaknesses of another. Ensemble models typically outperform individual algorithms because of their diversity. An automated machine learning platform should find the optimal algorithms to blend, include a diverse range of algorithms, and tune the weighting of the algorithms within each blender.

7. Head-to-Head Model Competitions

It's difficult to know ahead of time which algorithm will perform best in a particular modeling challenge, so it's necessary to compare the accuracy and speed of different algorithms on the data, regardless of the programming language or machine learning library the algorithms come from. A true automated machine learning platform must build and train dozens of algorithms, comparing the accuracy, speed, and individual predictions of each algorithm and then ranking the algorithms based on the needs of the business.

8. Human-Friendly Insights

Machine learning and AI have made massive strides in predictive power, but often at the price of complexity and interpretability. It's not enough for a model to score well on accuracy and speed – users must trust the answers. And in some industries, and even some geographies models must comply with regulations and be validated by a compliance team. Automated machine learning should describe model performance in a human-interpretable manner and provide easy-to-understand reasons for individual predictions to help an organization achieve compliance.

9. Easy Deployment

An analytics team can build an impressive predictive model, but it is of little use if the model is too complex for the IT team to reproduce, or if the business lacks the infrastructure to deploy the model to production. Easy, flexible deployment options are a hallmark of a workable automated machine learning solution, including APIs, exportable scoring code, and on-demand predictions that don't require the intervention of the IT team.

10. Model Monitoring and Management

Even the best models can go "stale" over time as conditions change or new sources of data become available. An ideal automated machine learning solution makes it easy to run a new model competition on the latest data, helping to determine if that model is still the best, or if there is a need to update the model. And as models change, the system should also be able to quickly update the documentation on the model to comply with regulatory requirements.

MACHINE LEARNING TOOLS

1| Amazon Lex

This service can be used for building conversational interfaces such as chatbots into any application using voice and text. You can easily build, test and deploy your chatbots directly from the service.

How It Works

This service provides advanced deep learning functionalities of automatic speech recognition for the conversion of speech to text, and NLP to recognise the intent of the text, enabling you to build highly engaging user experiences and lifelike conversational experiences.

2| Auto-WEKA

This is a data-mining tool that performs combined algorithm selection and hyper-parameter optimisation over the classification and regression algorithms that are being implemented in WEKA.

How It Works

When a dataset is given, this tool explores the hyperparameter settings for several algorithms and recommends the most preferred one to the user that gives good generalisation performance.

3| BigML

BigML is a comprehensive machine learning platform that provides a selection of machine learning algorithms to solve the real world problems by applying a single, standardised framework.

How It Works

This platform covers classification, regression, time series forecasting, cluster analysis, anomaly detection, topic modelling, and association discovery to facilitate unlimited predictive applications for various fields like agriculture, aerospace, healthcare, food, etc.

4| Data Robot

This is an automated machine learning platform by Kagglers to build and deploy accurate machine learning models for all levels of enthusiasts within a fraction of time.

How It Works

It enables the users to build and deploy highly accurate machine learning models by automatically detecting the best data pre-processing. It can employ encoding, scaling, text mining, etc. When the dataset is very large, it uses distributed algorithms to scale up the dataset.

5| Driverless AI

Driverless Ai is an artificial intelligence platform for automatic machine learning. The aim is to achieve the highest predictive accuracy in a shorter amount of time by end-to-end automation. It runs on commodity hardware and is designed to make use of GPUs, multi-GPU workstations, etc.

How It Works

This platform automates difficult machine learning workflows like feature engineering, model validation, tuning, selection as well as deployment. The model pipelines like feature engineering and models are exported as Python modules and Java standalone scoring artifacts.

6| Datawrapper

This is an open source platform that helps you generate visualisations like interactive graphs, maps, charts from your data within a short time. No design skills or code is required for it.

How It Works

The functionality in Datawrapper is provided by plugins. It works in three simple steps. Firstly, copy your data and paste it to the live-updating charts, then visualise it by customising and choosing the types of the charts and maps and finally, publish the ready-made chart as an image or pdf.

7| Fusioo

This is a database application where you can build tools you need. It gives you the freedom to create your own app to track, manage and share information without writing a single code.

How It Works

The steps are really easy. First, you create an app and name it according to your projector whatever you wish. Then, the next step is to create the Field that you need to track and finally a dashboard will be created for your apps. You can customise it by charts, lists, etc.

8| Google Cloud AutoML

Google Cloud AutoML is a suite of machine learning products that train high-quality custom machine learning models with minimum effort by leveraging Google's state-of-the-art transfer learning and Neural Architecture Search technology.

How It Works

It provides simple GUI for the users to train, evaluate, improve and deploy models based on your data. The data can be stored in the cloud storage. To generate a prediction on your trained model, just use the existing Vision API by adding a custom model.

9| IBM Watson Studio

This platform provides you tools for a hassle-free work with your own data to build and train models at scale with a faster optimisation. It helps to accelerate the machine learning workflows that are required to infuse artificial intelligence into your business or projects.

How It Works

The working process is easy and simple, You just have to go with the flow. First, choose a project type from the options provided, then define your project and store it into the cloud. Then you can customise by choosing several options like connect to a GitHub repository, link to a service, etc. and use it according to your project.

10| Microsoft Azure Machine Learning Studio

This is a browser-based machine platform that has a visual drag-and-drop environment that requires zero coding knowledge. It can be used by anyone regardless of the level of their skills.

How It Works

Firstly, you need to import your dataset from an excel sheet, etc. The data cleaning and other necessary pre-processing steps are performed. The data is split into training and testing sets and the built-in algorithms are applied to train the model and finally, your model will be scored, and you will get the predictions.

11| ML Jar

It is a human-first platform for machine learning that provides a service for prototyping, development and deploying pattern recognition algorithms.

How It Works

It includes three simple steps to build an accurate machine learning model. First, you need to upload the data with a secure connection, then training and tuning are done on many machine learning algorithms and the best match will be selected according to your data. Finally, use the best models for predictions and share your results.

12| Paxata

Paxata is an organisation that provides visual guidance, algorithmic intelligence, and smart suggestions, uses spark for enterprise data volumes, automatic governance, etc.

How It Works

The working process is simple here like you can use a wide range of sources to acquire data, performs data exploration using powerful visuals, performs data cleaning using normalisation of similar values using natural language processing, makes pivots on data, combining data frames by SmartFusion, etc.

13| Rapid Miner

This is an open sourced tool that helps in prediction modelling.

How It Works

It creates predictive models by using automated machine learning and data science best practices in just four clicks. This tool automatically analyses data to identify common quality problems like missing values. Then the best model for your data will be optimised by using multiple machine learning algorithms. The feature engineering is automated that lets you choose a balanced model and the predictive model is created.

14| Tableau

This has proved to be the most popular business intelligence and visualisation tool in the present scenario. You can create graphs, charts, maps, etc. within a short span of time.

How It Works

Various data sources can be connected in this tool and it has multiple options to represent data in different views, creating sets, applying filters, generating trend lines, forecasting, etc. You can deploy data drilling tools and explore various data that are available without any coding knowledge.

15| Trifacta

Trifacta provides as free stand-alone software that offers an intuitive GUI for performing data cleaning.

How It Works

This software takes data as input and evaluates a summary with multiple statistics by column and for each column, it recommends some transformations automatically. The data preparation can be done by various options present in the software like discovering, structure, cleaning, enriching, etc.

TOP REAL-LIFE EXAMPLES OF MACHINE LEARNING

Machine learning is one modern innovation that has helped man enhance not only many industrial and professional processes but also advances everyday living. But what is machine learning? It is a subset of artificial intelligence, which focuses on using statistical techniques to build intelligent computer systems in order to learn from databases available to it. Currently, machine learning has been used in multiple fields and industries. For example, medical diagnosis, image processing, prediction, classification, learning association, regression etc.

The intelligent systems built on machine learning algorithms have the capability to learn from past experience or historical data. Machine learning applications provide results on the basis of past experience. In this article, we will discuss 10 real-life examples of how machine learning is helping in creating better technology to power today's ideas.

Image Recognition

Image recognition is one of the most common uses of machine learning. There are many situations where you can classify the object as a digital image. For example, in the case of a black and white image, the intensity of each pixel is served as one of the measurements. In colored images, each pixel provides 3 measurements of intensities in three different colors – red, green and blue (RGB).

Machine learning can be used for face detection in an image as well. There is a separate category for each person in a database of several people. Machine learning is also used for character recognition to discern handwritten as well as printed letters. We can segment a piece of writing into smaller images, each containing a single character.

Speech Recognition

Speech recognition is the translation of spoken words into the text. It is also known as computer speech recognition or automatic speech recognition. Here, a software application can recognize the words spoken in an audio clip or file, and then subsequently convert the audio into a text file. The measurement in this application can be a set of numbers that represent the speech signal. We can also segment the speech signal by intensities in different time-frequency bands.

Speech recognition is used in the applications like voice user interface, voice searches and more. Voice user interfaces include voice dialing, call routing, and appliance control. It can also be used a simple data entry and the preparation of structured documents.

Medical diagnosis

Machine learning can be used in the techniques and tools that can help in the diagnosis of diseases. It is used for the analysis of the clinical parameters and their combination for the prognosis example prediction of disease progression for the extraction of medical knowledge for the outcome research, for therapy planning and patient monitoring. These are the successful implementations of the machine learning methods. It can help in the integration of computer-based systems in the healthcare sector.

Statistical Arbitrage

In finance, arbitrage refers to the automated trading strategies that are of a short-term and involve a large number of securities. In these strategies, the user focuses on implementing the trading algorithm for a set of securities on the basis of quantities like historical correlations and the general economic variables. Machine learning methods are applied to obtain an index arbitrage strategy. We apply linear regression and the Support Vector Machine to the prices of a stream of stocks.

Learning associations

Learning associations is the process of developing insights into the various associations between the products. A good example is how the unrelated products can be associated with one another. One of the applications of machine learning is studying the associations between the products that people buy. If a person buys a product, he will be shown similar products because there is a relation between the two products. When any new products are launched in the market, they are associated with the old ones to increase their sales.

Classification

A classification is a process of placing each individual under study in many classes. Classification helps to analyze the measurements of an object to identify the category to which that object belongs. To establish an efficient relation, analysts use data. For example, before a bank decides to distribute loans, it assesses the customers on their ability to pay loans. By considering the factors like customer's earnings, savings, and financial history, we can do it. This information is taken from the past data on the loan.

Prediction

Machine learning can also be used in the prediction systems. Considering the loan example, to compute the probability of a fault, the system will need to classify the available data in groups. It is defined by a set of rules prescribed by the analysts. Once the classification is done, we can calculate the probability of the fault. These computations can compute across all the sectors for varied purposes. Making predictions is one of the best machine learning applications.

Extraction

Extraction of information is one of the best applications of machine learning. It is the process of extracting structured information from the unstructured data. For example, the web pages, articles, blogs, business reports, and emails. The relational database maintains the output produced by the information extraction. The process of extraction takes a set of documents as input and outputs the structured data.

Regression

We can also implement machine learning in the regression as well. In regression, we can use the principle of machine learning to optimize the parameters. It can also be used to decrease the approximation error and calculate the closest possible outcome. We can also use the machine learning for the function optimization. We can also choose to alter the inputs in order to get the closest possible outcome.

Financial Services

Machine learning has a lot of potential in the financial and banking sector. It is the driving force behind the popularity of the financial services. Machine learning can help the banks, financial institutions to make smarter decisions. Machine learning can help the financial services to spot an account closure before it occurs. It can also track the spending pattern of the customers. Machine learning can also perform the market analysis. Smart machines can be trained to track the spending patterns. The algorithms can identify the trends easily and can react in real time.

In a nutshell, we can say that machine learning is an incredible breakthrough in the field of artificial intelligence. And while machine learning has some frightening implications, these machine learning applications are one of the ways through which technology can improve our lives.

WAYS MACHINE LEARNING WILL IMPACT YOUR EVERYDAY LIFE

Artificial intelligence (AI) and machine learning is now considered to be one of the biggest innovations since the microchip. AI used to be a fanciful concept from science fiction, but now it's becoming a daily reality. Neural networks (imitating the process of real neurons in the brain) are paving the way toward breakthroughs in machine learning, called "deep learning."

Machine learning can help us live happier, healthier, and more productive lives... if we know how to harness its power.

Some say that AI is ushering in another "industrial revolution." Whereas the previous Industrial Revolution harnessed physical and mechanical strength, this new revolution will harness mental and cognitive ability. One day, computers will not only replace manual labor, but also mental labor. But how exactly will this happen? And is it already happening?

1. Intelligent Gaming

Some of you may remember 1997 when IBM's Deep Blue defeated Gary Kasparov in chess. But if you weren't old enough then, you might remember when another computer program, Google DeepMind's AlphaGo, defeated Lee Sedol, the Go world champion, in 2016.

Go is an ancient Chinese game, much more difficult for computers to master than chess. But AlphaGo was specifically trained to play Go, not by simply analyzing the moves of the very best players, but by learning how to play the game better from practicing against itself millions of times.

2. Self-Driving Cars and Automated Transportation

Have you flown on an airplane lately? If so, then you've already experienced transportation automation at work. These modern commercial aircraft use FMS (Flight Management System), a combination of GPS, motion sensors, and computer systems to track its position during flight. So an average Boeing 777 pilot spends just seven minutes actually flying the plane manually, and many of those minutes are spent during takeoff and landing.

The leap into self-driving cars is more complicated. There are more cars on the road, obstacles to avoid, and limitations to account for in terms of traffic patterns and rules. Even so, self-driving cars are already a reality. These AI-powered cars have even surpassed human-driven cars in safety, according to a study with 55 Google vehicles that have driven over 1.3 million miles altogether.

The navigation question has already been solved long ago. Google Maps already sources location data from your smartphone. By comparing the location of a device from one point in time to another, it can determine how fast the device is traveling. Put simply, it can determine how slow traffic is in real time. It can combine that data with incidents reported by users to build a picture of the traffic at any given moment. Maps can recommend the fastest route for you based on traffic jams, construction work or accidents between you and your destination.

But what about the skill of actually driving a car? Well, machine learning allows self-driving cars to instantaneously adapt to changing road conditions, while at the same time learning from new road situations. By continuously parsing through a stream of visual and sensor data, onboard computers can make split-second decisions even faster than well-trained drivers.

It's not magic. It's based on the exact same fundamentals of machine learning used in other industries. You have input features (i.e. the real-time visual and sensor data) and an output (i.e. a decision among the universe of possible next "actions" for a car).

So, sure these self-driving cars already exist, but are they ready for prime-time? Perhaps not yet, since the vehicles are currently required to have a driver present for safety. So despite exciting developments in this new field of automated transportation, the technology isn't perfect yet. But give it a few months or years, and you'll probably want to have one of these cars yourself.

3. Cyborg Technology

Obviously, our bodies and our brains have built in limitations and weaknesses. Technology will improve to to such an extent that we will be able to augment some of our weaknesses and limitations with computers, thereby enhancing many of our natural abilities.

But wait - before you start picturing dystopian worlds of steel and flesh, consider for a moment that most people walking around are already "cyborgs" in a sense.

How many people do you know who could survive the day without their trusty smartphone? We already rely on these handheld computers for communication, navigation, acquiring knowledge, receiving important news, and a host of other activities.

4. Taking Over Dangerous Jobs

One of the most dangerous jobs is bomb disposal. Today, robots (or more technically, drones) are taking over these risky jobs, among others. Right now, most of these drones require a human to control them. But as machine learning technology improves in the future, these tasks would be done completely by robots with AI. This technology alone has already saved thousands of lives.

Another job being outsourced to robots is welding. This kind of work produces noise, intense heat, and toxic substances found in the fumes. Without machine learning, these robot welders would need to be pre-programmed to weld in a certain location. However, advancements in computer vision and deep learning have enabled more flexibility and greater accuracy.

5. Environmental Protection

Machines can store and access more data than any one person could—including mind-boggling statistics. Using big data, AI could one day identify trends and use that information to arrive at h solutions to previously untenable problems.

For example, IBM's Green Horizon Project analyzes environmental data from thousands of sensors and sources to product accurate, evolving weather and pollution forecasts. It allows city planners to run "what-if" scenarios and model ways to mitigate environmental impact.

And that's just beginning. Exciting environment-oriented innovations are entering the market every day, from self-adjusting smart thermostats to distributed energy grids.

6. Digital Empathy and Robots as Friends

Most robots are still emotionless. But a company in Japan has made the first big steps toward a robot companion—one that can understand and feel emotions. Introduced in 2014, Pepper the companion robot went on sale in 2015, with all 1,000 initial units selling out within a minute. The robot was programmed to read human emotions, develop its own, and help its human friends stay happy.

"Practical advancements in artificial intelligence will start to enable a more contextual form of computing with some of our devices, particularly smartphones and smart speakers... part of the way this development will likely occur is by learning more about people and how they think—essentially building a form of digital empathy."

As funny as it sounds, the day that one can literally "buy a friend" is not too far away.

7. Improved Elder Care

For many seniors, everyday tasks can be a struggle. Many have to hire outside help or rely on family members. Elder care is a growing concern for many families.

AI is at a stage where replacing this need isn't too far off. Elderly relatives who don't want to leave their homes could be assisted by in-home robots. That solution offers family members more flexibility in managing a loved one's care. These robots could help seniors with everyday tasks and allow them to stay independent and living in their homes for as long as possible, improving their overall well-being.

Medical and AI researchers have even piloted systems based on infrared cameras that can detect when an elderly person falls. Researchers and medical specialists can also monitor alcohol and food consumption, fevers, restlessness, urinary frequency, chair and bed comfort, fluid intake, eating, sleeping, declining mobility, and more.

8. Enhanced Health Care

Hospitals may soon put your wellbeing in the hands of an AI, and that's good news. Hospitals that utilize machine learning to aid in treating patients see fewer accidents and fewer cases of hospital-related illnesses, like sepsis. AI is also tackling some of medicine's most intractable problems, such as allowing researchers to better understand genetic diseases through the use of predictive models.

Previously, health professionals must review reams of data manually before they diagnose or treat a patient. Today, high-performance computing GPUs have become key tools for deep learning and AI platforms. Deep learning models quickly provide real-time insights and, combined with the explosion of computing power, are helping healthcare professionals diagnose patients faster and more accurately, develop innovative new drugs and treatments, reduce medical and diagnostic errors, predict adverse reactions, and lower the costs of healthcare for providers and patients.

9. Innovations in Banking

Consider how many people have a bank account. Now, on top of that, consider the number of credit cards that are in circulation. How many man hours would it take for employees to sift through the thousands of transactions that take place every day? By the time they noticed an anomaly, your bank account could be empty or your credit card maxed out.

Using location data and purchase patterns, AI can also help banks and credit issuers identify fraudulent behavior while it is happening. These machine learning based anomaly detection models monitor transaction requests. They can spot patterns in your transactions and alert users to suspicious activity.

They can even confirm with you that the purchase was indeed yours before they process the payment. It may seem inconvenient if it was just you eating at a restaurant while traveling on holiday, but it could end up saving you thousands of dollars someday.

10. Personalized Digital Media

Machine learning has massive potential in the entertainment industry, and the technology has already found a home in streaming services such as Netflix, Amazon Prime, Spotify, and Google Play. Some algorithms are already being used to eliminate buffering and low-quality playback, getting you the best quality from your internet service provider.

ML algorithms are also making use of the almost endless stream of data about consumers' viewing habits, helping streaming services offer more useful recommendations.

They will help more and more with the production of media too. NLP (Natural Language Processing) algorithms help write trending news stories to decrease production time, and a new MIT-developed AI named Shelley is helps users write horror stories through deep learning algorithms and a bank of user-generated fiction. At this rate, the next great content creators may not be human at all.

11. Home Security and Smart Homes

For the best tech in home security, many homeowners look toward AI-integrated cameras and alarm systems. These cutting-edge systems use facial recognition software and machine learning to build a catalog of your home's frequent visitors, allowing these systems to detect uninvited guests in an instant.

AI-powered smart homes also provide many other useful features, like tracking when you last walked the dog or notifying you when your kids come home from school. The newest systems can even call for emergency services autonomously, making it an attractive alternative to subscription-based services that provide similar benefits.

Consumer AI will enable wave after wave of convenient automations in the home. When combined with appliances, AI could make housework and household management seamless.

AI-powered apps which allow the oven to communicate with the refrigerator and the pantry robot would act like home chefs. Instant replenishment of food and supplies would mean never running out of anything again. Cleaning could be schedule through sensor-to-appliance connections, after which robotic cleaners would work almost completely independently of humans.

Another advantage of smart homes would be a reduction of household waste and automated recycling, putting the household in better balance with the ecosystem. Releasing humans from housework could deliver major benefits in terms of improving sustainability, saving time, and reducing stress.

12. Streamlined Logistics and Distribution

Imagine getting a package in just a few hours and at a very low shipping cost. That's the promise of AI in logistics and distribution, with its promise to tame the massive amounts of data and decisions in the trillion-dollar shipping and logistics industry. Amazon has already started experimenting with autonomous drones that blow their already-quite-fast two-day shipping out of the water.

Currently, shipping costs are still quite expensive. Improving efficiency through AI integration and automation will mean big reductions in shipping costs and increases in delivery speed. Optimization opportunities in supply chain management, vehicle maintenance, and inventory will also make shipping faster, easier, and more environmentally friendly.

13. Digital Personal Assistants

Imagine never needing to worry about preparing dinner, because your personal assistant knows what you like, what you have in your pantry, and which days of the week you like to cook at home. Imagine that when you get back from work, all your groceries are waiting at your doorstep, ready for you to prepare that delicious meal you've been craving. You even have a bonus recipe for a new dessert you've been meaning to try.

Digital assistants are getting smarter by the year. Companies such as Amazon and Google are pouring billions of dollars into making digital assistants even better at speech recognition and learning about our daily routines, opening the door to more and more complex tasks.

14. Brick and Mortar and AI

While some people claim that e-commerce and the Internet will completely eat away the traditional retail market, the more likely scenario is that they will arrive at some sort of equilibrium. However, it's undeniable that even the biggest traditional retail giants are starting to adopt AI-powered technologies to gain a competitive edge.

15. Customized News and Market Reports

Can you imagine getting market reports that were written on demand for you and not just when the market closed?

Instead of a generic recap of market performance, your customized report compares how your portfolio performed against the broader market, citing key reasons why. For example: "It's 3:14 pm. The market is currently up 2%, but your portfolio is down 3%. This is attributed in part to the purchase of XYZ stock last week, which has fallen sharply since ..."

While the most obvious application of this technology would be in the finance and investing space, there are plenty of other domains that would benefit as well, including ad tech, agriculture, sports, and more.

As many people have wisely observed, the dream of artificial intelligence is not new. It has been around since the very earliest days of computing. Pioneers have always imagined ways to build intelligent learning machines.

Currently, most promising approach of AI is the use of applied machine learning. Rather than trying to encode machines with everything they need to know up front (which is impossible), we want to enable them to learn, and then to learn how to learn.

Machine learning's time has come, and it is in the process of revolutionizing all of our lives.

TOP BEST MACHINE LEARNING APPLICATIONS IN REAL WORLD

The magical touch of mysterious science makes our life more comfortable and preferable than before. In our everyday life, the contribution of science is just undeniable. We cannot overlook or ignore the effect of science in our life. Since, at present, we are habituated to the Internet in many steps of our day to day life, i.e., to go through an unknown route now we use a Google map, to express our thoughts or feelings use social networks, or to share our knowledge use blogs, to know the news we use online news portals and so on. If we try to understand the effect of science in our life precisely, then we will notice that actually, these are the outcome of using Artificial Intelligence and Machine Learning applications. In this article, we try to capture the splendid real-time applications of Machine Learning which will make our perception of life more digital.

1. Image Recognition

Image Recognition is one of the most significant Machine Learning applications. Basically, it is an approach for identifying and detecting a feature or an object in the digital image. Moreover, this technique can be used for further analysis such as pattern recognition, face detection, face recognition, optical character recognition and many more.

Though several techniques are available, using a machine learning approach for image recognition is preferable. In a machine learning approach for image-recognition is involved extracting the key features from the image and therefore input these features to a machine learning model.

2. Sentiment Analysis

Sentiment analysis is another real-time machine learning application. It also refers to opinion mining, sentiment classification, etc. It's a process of determining the attitude or opinion of the speaker or the writer. In other words, it's the process of finding out the emotion from the text.

The main concern of sentiment analysis is " what other people think?". Assume that someone writes 'the movie is not so good.' To find out the actual thought or opinion from the text (is it good or bad) is the task of sentiment analysis. This sentiment analysis application can also apply to the further application such as in review based website, decision-making application.

The machine learning approach is a discipline that constructs a system by extracting the knowledge from data. Additionally, this approach can use big data to develop a system. In machine learning approach there are two types of learning algorithm supervised and unsupervised. Both of these can be used to sentiment analysis.

3. News Classification

News classification is another benchmark application of a machine learning approach. Why or How? As a matter of fact that now the volume of information has grown tremendously on the web. However, every person has his individual interest or choice. So, to pick or gather a piece of appropriate information becomes a challenge to the users from the ocean of this web.

Providing that interesting category of news to the target readers will surely increase the acceptability of news sites. Moreover, readers or users can search for specific news effectively and efficiently.

There are several methods of machine learning in this purpose, i.e., support vector machine, naive Bayes, k-nearest neighbor, etc. Moreover, there are several "news classification software" is available.

4. Video Surveillance

A small video file contains more information compared to text documents and other media files such as audio, images. For this reason, extracting useful information from video, i.e., the automated video surveillance system has become a hot research issue. With this regard, video surveillance is one of the advanced application of a machine learning approach.

The presence of a human in a different frame of a video is a common scenario. In the security-based application, identification of the human from the videos is an important issue. The face pattern is the most widely used parameter to recognize a person.

A system with the ability to gather information about the presence of the same person in a different frame of a video is highly demanding. There are several methods of machine learning algorithm to track the movement of human and identifying them.

5. Email Classification and Spam Filtering

To classify email and filter the spam in an automatic way machine learning algorithm is employed. There are many techniques, i.e., multi-layer perception, C4.5 decision tree induction, are used to filter the spam. The rule-based spam filtering has some drawbacks to filter the spam whereas spam filtering using the ML approach is more efficient.

6. Speech Recognition

Speech recognition is the process of transforming spoken words into text. It is additionally called automatic speech recognition, computer speech recognition or speech to text. This field is benefited from the advancement of machine learning approach and big data.

At present, all commercial purpose speech recognition system uses a machine learning approach to recognize the speech. Why? The speech recognition system using machine learning approach outperforms better than the speech recognition system using a traditional method.

Because, in a machine learning approach, the system is trained before it goes for the validation. Basically, the machine learning software of speech recognition works two learning phases: 1. Before the software purchase (train the software in an independent speaker domain) 2. After the user purchases the software (train the software in a speaker dependent domain).

This application can also be used for further analysis, i.e., health care domain, educational, and military.

7. Online Fraud Detection

Online fraud detection is an advanced application of machine learning algorithm. This approach is practical to provide cybersecurity to the users efficiently. Recently, PayPal is using a machine learning algorithm for money laundering. This advanced machine learning application helps to reduce the loss and maximize the profit. Using machine learning in this application, the detection system becomes robust than any other traditional rule-based system.

8. Classification

Classification or categorization is the process of classifying the objects or instances into a set of predefined classes. The use of machine learning approach makes a classifier system more dynamic. The goal of the ML approach is to build a concise model. This approach is to help to improve the efficiency of a classifier system.

Every instance in a data set used by the machine learning algorithm is represented using the same set of features. These instances may have a known label; this is called the supervised machine learning algorithm. In contrast, if the labels are known then its called the unsupervised. These two variations of the machine learning approaches are used for classification problems.

9. Author Identification

With the rapid growth of the Internet, the illegal use of online messages for inappropriate or illegal purposes has become a major concern for society. For this regard, author identification is required.

Author identification also is known as authorship identification. The author identification system may use a variety of fields such as criminal justice, academia, and anthropology. Additionally, organizations like Thorn use author identification to help end the circulation of child sexual abuse material on the web and bring justice to a child.

10. Prediction

Prediction is the process of saying something based on the previous history. It can be weather prediction, traffic prediction and may more. All sort of forecasts can be done using a machine learning approach. There are several methods like Hidden Markov model can be used for prediction.

11. Regression

Regression is another application of machine learning. There are several techniques for regression is available.

Suppose, X1, X2, X3 ,....Xn are the input variables, and Y is the output. During this case, using machine learning technology to provide the output (y) on the idea of the input variables (x). A model is used to precise the connection between numerous parameters as below:

$Y=g(x)$

Using machine learning approach in regression, the parameters can be optimized.

12. Services of Social Media

Social media is using the machine learning approach to create attractive and splendid features, i.e. people you may know, suggestion, react options for their users. These features are just an outcome of the machine learning technique.

Do you ever think of how they use the machine learning approach to engage you in your social account? For example, Facebook continuously notices your activities like with whom you chat, your likes, workplace, study place. And machine learning always acts based on experience. So, Facebook gives you a suggestion based on your activities.

13. Medical Services

Machine learning methods, tools are used extensively in the area of medical related problem. As an instance to detect a disease, therapy planning, medical-related research, prediction of the disease situation. Using machine learning based software in the healthcare problem brings a breakthrough in our medical science.

14. Recommendation for Products and Services

Suppose that; we purchased several things from an online shop several days before. After a couple of days, you will notice that the related shopping websites or services are recommended for you.

Again, if you search something in google therefore after your searching, the similar type of things are recommended for you. This recommendation of products and services are the advance application of machine learning technique.

Several machine learning methods like supervised, semi-supervised, unsupervised, reinforcement are used to develop these products recommendation based system. This type of system also built with the incorporation of big data and machine learning technique.

15. Online Customer Supports

Recently almost all websites allow the customer to chat with the website representative. However, not website has an executive. Basically, they develop a chat-bot to chat with the customer to know their opinion. This is possible only for the machine learning approach. It's just a beauty of machine learning algorithm.

16. Age/Gender Identification

The recently forensic related task has become a hot research issue in the world of research. Many researchers are working for bringing an effective and efficient system to develop an enriched system.

In this context, age or gender identification is an important task for many cases. Age or gender identification can be done using a machine learning algorithm, i.e. using SVM classifier.

17. Language Identification

Language identification (Language Guessing) is the process of identifying the type of language. Apache

OpenNLP, Apache Tika is the language identifying software. There are several approaches to identify the language. Among these, the machine learning approach is efficient.

18. Information Retrieval

The most significant machine learning approach is information retrieval. It is the process of extracting the knowledge or structured data from the unstructured data. Since, now the availability of information has been grown tremendously for web blogs, website, and social media.

Information retrieval plays a vital role in the big data sector. In a machine learning approach, a set of unstructured data is taken for input and therefore extracts the knowledge from the data.

19. Robot Control

A machine learning algorithm is used in a variety of robot control system. For instance, recently several types of research have been working to gain control over stable helicopter flight and helicopter aerobatics.

In Darpa-sponsored competition, a robot driving for over one hundred miles within the desert was won by a robot that used machine learning to refine its ability to notice distant objects.

20. Virtual Personal Assistant

A virtual personal assistant is the advanced application of machine learning applications. In the machine learning technique, this system acts as follows: a machine-learning based system takes input, and processes the input and gives the resultant output. The machine learning approach is important as they act based on the experience.

The field machine learning works for the development and application of real-time problems which makes our life more easy to survive and modern. The main difference between the traditional software and machine learning based software is that the system is trained using a large volume of data. Also, it acts based on experience. So, the machine learning approach is effective than the traditional approach in problem-solving.

CUSTOMER CHURN PREDICTION USING MACHINE LEARNING: MAIN APPROACHES AND MODELS

What is customer churn?

Customer churn (or customer attrition) is a tendency of customers to abandon a brand and stop being a paying client of a particular business. The percentage of customers that discontinue using a company's products or services during a particular time period is called a customer churn (attrition) rate. One of the ways to calculate a churn rate is to divide the number of customers lost during a given time interval by the number of acquired customers, and then multiply that number by 100 percent. For example, if you got 150 customers and lost three last month, then your monthly churn rate is 2 percent.

Churn rate is a health indicator for businesses whose customers are subscribers and paying for services on a recurring basis, "Customers [of subscription-driven businesses] opt for a product or a service for a particular period, which can be rather short – say, a month. Thus, a customer stays open for more interesting or advantageous offers. Plus, each time their current commitment ends, customers have a chance to reconsider and choose not to continue with the company. Of course, some natural churn is inevitable, and the figure differs from industry to industry. But having a higher churn figure than that is a definite sign that a business is doing something wrong."

There are many things brands may do wrong, from complicated onboarding when customers aren't given easy-to-understand information about product usage and its capabilities to poor communication, e.g. the lack of feedback or delayed answers to queries. Another situation: Longtime clients may feel unappreciated because they don't get as many bonuses as the new ones.

In general, it's the overall customer experience that defines brand perception and influences how customers recognize value for money of products or services they use.

The reality is that even loyal customers won't tolerate a brand if they've had one or several issues with it. For instance, 59 percent of US respondents to the survey by PricewaterhouseCoopers (PwC) noted that they will say goodbye to a brand after several bad experiences, and 17 percent of them after just one bad experience.

Impact of customer churn on businesses

Well, churn is bad. But how exactly does it affect company performance in the long run?

Don't underestimate the impact of even a tiny percentage of churn. "In a subscription-based business, even a small rate of monthly/quarterly churn will compound quickly over time. Just 1 percent monthly churn translates to almost 12 percent yearly churn. Given that it's far more expensive to acquire a new customer than to retain an existing one, businesses with high churn rates will quickly find themselves in a financial hole as they have to devote more and more resources to new customer acquisition."

Many surveys focusing on customer acquisition and retention costs are available online. Getting a new customer may cost up to five times more than retaining an existing customer.

Churn rates do correlate with lost revenue and increased acquisition spend. In addition, they play a more nuanced role in a company's growth potential, "Today's buyers aren't shy about sharing their experiences with vendors through channels like review sites and social media, as well as peer-to-peer networks. Research found that 49 percent of buyers reported sharing an experience they had with a company on social media. In a world of eroding trust in businesses, word of mouth plays a more critical role in the buying process than ever before. From the same Research study, 55 percent of buyers no longer trust the companies they buy from as much as they used to, 65 percent don't trust company press releases, 69 percent don't trust advertisements, and 71 percent don't trust sponsored ads on social networks."

Companies with high churn rates aren't only failing to deliver in their relationships with ex-customers but also damage their future acquisition efforts by creating negative word-of-mouth around their products.

Churn rate is one of the critical performance indicators for subscription businesses. The subscription business model – pioneered by English book publishers in the 17th century – is very popular among modern service providers. Let's take a quick look at these companies:

Music and video streaming services are probably the most commonly associated with the subscription business model (Netflix, YouTube, Apple Music, Google Play, Spotify, Hulu, Amazon Video, Deezer, etc.).

Media. Digital presence is a must among the press, so news companies offer readers digital subscriptions besides print ones (Bloomberg, The Guardian, Financial Times, The New York Times, Medium etc.).

Telecom companies (cable or wireless). These companies may provide a full range of products and services, including wireless network, internet, TV, cell phone, and home phone services (AT&T, Sprint, Verizon, Cox Communications, etc.). Some specialize in mobile telecommunications (China Mobile, Vodafone, T-Mobile, etc.).

Software as a service providers. The adoption of cloud-hosted software is growing. The SaaS market remains the largest segment of the cloud market. Its revenue is expected to grow 17.8 percent and reach $85.1 billion in 2019. The product range of SaaS providers is extensive: graphic and video editing (Adobe Creative Cloud, Canva), accounting (Sage 50cloud, FreshBooks), eCommerce (BigCommerce, Shopify), email marketing (MailChimp, Zoho Campaigns), and many others.

These company types may use churn rate to measure the effectiveness of cross-department operations and product management.

Identifying at-risk customers with machine learning: problem-solving at a glance

Companies that constantly monitor how people engage with products, encourage clients to share opinions, and solve their issues promptly have greater opportunities to maintain mutually beneficial client relationships.

And now imagine a company that has been gathering customer data for a while, so it can use it to identify behavior patterns of potential churners, segment these at-risk customers, and take appropriate actions to gain back their trust. Those following a proactive approach to customer churn management use predictive analytics. That's one of four analytics types that entails forecasting the probability of future outcomes, events, or values by analyzing current and historical data. Predictive analytics utilizes various statistical techniques, such as data mining (pattern recognition) and machine learning (ML).

"The one weakness of tracking just real churn is that it serves only as a lagging indicator of poor customer experience, which is where a predictive churn model becomes extremely valuable".

The main trait of machine learning is building systems capable of finding patterns in data, learning from it without explicit programming. In the context of customer churn prediction, these are online behavior characteristics that indicate decreasing customer satisfaction from using company services/products.

Detecting customers at risk of churn helps take measures in advance

"As to identifying potential churners, machine learning algorithms can do a great job here. They reveal some shared behavior patterns of those customers who have already left the company. Then, ML algorithms check the behavior of current customers against such patterns and signal if they discover potential churners."

Subscription-based businesses leverage ML for predictive analytics to find out which current users aren't fully satisfied with their services and address their issues when it's not too late: "Identifying customers at risk of churn as many as 11 months before their renewal enables our customer success team to engage these customers, understand their pain points, and with them, put together a long term plan focused on helping the customer realize value from the service they bought".

Use cases for predictive churn modeling go beyond proactive engagement with prospective churning customers and selecting effective retention actions. ML-based software allows customer success managers to define which customers they should contact. In other words, employees can be sure they're speaking with the right customers at the right time.

Sales, customer success, and marketing teams can also use the knowledge from the data analysis to align their actions. "For example, if a customer is showing signs of churn risk, that's probably not a great time for sales to reach out with information about additional services the customer might be interested in. Rather, that engagement should be with the CSM so they can help the customer become re-engaged and see value in the products they currently have. Like sales, marketing can engage with customers differently depending on their current indication of churn risk: For example, non-churn risk customers are better candidates to participate in a case study than a customer who is currently a churn risk". Generally speaking, the strategy of customer interaction should be based on ethics and sense of timing. And using machine learning for customer data analysis can bring insights to power this strategy.

Predicting customer churn with machine learning

As with any machine learning task, data science specialists first need data to work with. Depending on the goal, researchers define what data they must collect. Next, selected data is prepared, preprocessed, and transformed in a form suitable for building machine learning models. Finding the right methods to training machines, fine-tuning the models, and selecting the best performers is another significant part of the work. Once a model that makes predictions with the highest accuracy is chosen, it can be put into production.

Understanding a problem and a final goal

It's important to understand what insights one needs to get from the analysis. In short, you must decide what question to ask and consequently what type of machine learning problem to solve: classification or regression. Sounds complicated, but bear with us.

Classification. The goal of classification is to determine to which class or category a data point (customer in our case) belongs to. For classification problems, data scientists would use historical data with predefined target variables AKA labels (churner/non-churner) – answers that need to be predicted – to train an algorithm. With classification, businesses can answer the following questions:

Will this customer churn or not?

Will a customer renew their subscription?

Will a user downgrade a pricing plan?

Are there any signs of unusual customer behavior?

The fourth question about atypical behavior signs represents a type of a classification problem called anomaly detection. Anomaly detection is about identifying outliers – data points that significantly deviate from the rest of the data.

Regression.

Customer churn prediction can be also formulated as a regression task. Regression analysis is a statistical technique to estimate the relationship between a target variable and other data values that influence the target variable, expressed in continuous values. If that's too hard – the result of regression is always some number, while classification always suggests a category. In addition, regression analysis allows for estimating how many different variables in data influence a target variable. With regression, businesses can forecast in what period of time a specific customer is likely to churn or receive some probability estimate of churn per customer.

Data collection

Identifying data sources. Once you've identified which kinds of insights to look for, you can decide what data sources are necessary for further predictive modeling. Let's assume the most common sources of data you can use for predicting churn:

CRM systems (including sales and customer support records)

Analytics services (e.g., Google Analytics, AWStats, CrazyEgg)

Feedback on social media and review platforms

Feedback provided on request for your organization, etc.

Obviously, the list may be longer or shorter depending on the industry.

Data preparation and preprocessing

Historical data that was selected for solving the problem must be transformed into a format suitable for machine learning. Since model performance and therefore the quality of received insights depend on the quality of data, the primary aim is to make sure all data points are presented using the same logic, and the overall dataset is free of inconsistencies. Previously we wrote an article about basic techniques for dataset preparation, so feel free to check it out if you want to know more on the topic.

Feature engineering, extraction, and selection. Feature engineering is a very important part of dataset preparation. During the process, data scientists create a set of attributes (input features) that represent various behavior patterns related to customer engagement level with a service or product. In a broad sense, features are measurable characteristics of observations that an ML model takes into account to predict outcomes (in our case the decision relates to churn probability.)

Although behavior characteristics are specific to each industry, approaches to identifying at-risk customers are universal: "A business looks for specific behavior patterns that reveal potential churners."

TACKLING CHURN USING MACHINE LEARNING

Customer Churn (attrition) is a term used in business to denote an existing customer that stops using or buying a company's services or products. Churn is a classic issue for all companies doing business; it is an important point that deserves their full attention as brand loyalty means better sales and turnover. All businesses in all sectors use a variety of methods to measure KPI and metrics that assess customers churn propensity and attempt to infer customers motivation for attrition and then better address their needs.

Churn factors

There are diverse factors that worsen churn rate and make it higher :

In churn we have two kind of behavior, [1] the customer quit and resign his contract with the company, which is the standard and traditional way and [2] the customer doesn't quit but at the same time he doesn't use the service of product (or rarely), this is what we call dormancy. A dormant customer has not churned yet, but he has not generated any revenue within a given time frame before churn. so dormancy Prediction Modelling tries to prevent customer inactivity.

These two approaches must be taken into account while tackling churn, to put good criteria that define a churner, the idea is that the more your customers interact with your business, the smaller the churn rate will be. for example:

- In Baking: a churner would be a person who does not put and does not transfer or receive money into his bank account for at least 2 months.

- In E-commerce: a churner would be a person who does not make any order and does interact with companies campaigns for at least 3 Months.

- In Telecom: a churner would be a person who does not make calls, SMS, data connection or receives calls for at least 1 Month.

Churn can be customer dormancy or contract termination

Preventing churn using Machine learning

Churn must be treated before it becomes clearly apparent, that is why machine learning methods are used for their predictive power, they allow to create more sophisticated and effective algorithms to reduce churn. The idea is to exploit customer's information and activity (by using historical data of churners and non-churners) to train models to recognize those who are likely to quit and separate active users from a dormant user. Here the types of historical information used as an input to train machine learning models:

To tackle Churn, three main machine learning methods are used:

I. Classification:

Use methods like SVM, logistic regression or neural network to estimate likelihood/score that customers will churn and then address the risky population by prioritizing those who have a higher profitability and churn rate.

Classification example: Neural network

Neural network is a black-box method inspired by the human brain. It is based on an architecture composed of multiple non-linear layers of neurons (parameters weights and biases) whose objective is to learn hierarchical features. Each neuron performs a combination of its inputs, which allows neurons from the next layer to separate classes with a non-linear curve and not a simple line. The deeper the layers, the more complex the learned features are.

Artificial neural network can be used to classify churners from non-churners

Process of learning use loss function like Mean Square Error MSE or Cross entropy CE to measure how well the neural network performs to map training examples to correct output, and then tweak his parameters (weights and biases) using gradient descent and backpropagation process.

II. Survival analysis:

Survival analysis use methods like Cox regression to analyze the estimate the time of occurrence of an event (like the churn event), and infers the shelf life as a customer.

II.1. Survival analysis example: Cox Regression

Cox regression is a multivariate survival analysis regression method used first in the medical field for investigating the effect of several variables on the time of occurrence of a given event (death for medical field an in our case the event is customer churn). It uses the hazard function h(t) which is the probability that a customer churn happens at a particular time t, with (b1,...,bp) coefficients that measure the effect size of variables (x1,...,xp):

III. Cluster Migration Analysis:

Cluster Migration Analysis is based on clustering analysis, it segment the customer's population into loyalty profiles of different level (e.g. very loyal, moderately loyal, risky, very risky), and then investigates changes of cluster membership through time, that are due to change in data provoked by events, like new offers, promotions, marketing campaigns, or churn propensity that influence customer's behaviors. Analyzing these changes over a period helps to better understand usage patterns and churn signals such as abrupt clustering changes and analyze which attributes changed most significantly and trigger clustering migration.

Cluster migration analysis through time

Dealing with Churn is a hard task and most of time executives and marketers want to have an accurate target, so these three Machine learning methods can be combined to higher the accuracy of the churn prediction rate.

The primary source of income for all businesses are their customers, so the existing customers are their most important assets, retaining them become a real goal and building customer loyalty is considered to deserve all the efforts.

Machine learning is used to detect future churners but is not a magical remedy, it only helps to enhance the loyalty management process by providing a better customer segmentation and more accurate targets which give a head start to marketers to influence the churn decision using targeted communication campaigns including special offers, bonuses, and promotions.

WAYS MACHINE LEARNING IS REVOLUTIONIZING SALES

AI and machine learning technologies excel at pattern recognition, enabling sales teams to find the highest potential new prospects by matching data profiles with their most valuable customers. Nearly all AI-enabled CRM applications are providing the ability to define a series of attributes, characteristics and their specific values that pinpoint the highest potential prospects. Selecting and prioritizing new prospects using this approach saves sales teams thousands of hours a year.

Lead scoring and nurturing based on AI and machine learning algorithms help guide sales and marketing teams to turn Marketing Qualified Leads (MQL) into Sales Qualified Leads (SQL), strengthening sales pipelines in the process. One of the most important areas of collaboration between sales and marketing is lead nurturing strategies that move prospects through the pipeline. AI and machine learning are enriching the collaboration with insights from third-party data, prospect's activity at events and on the website, and from previous conversations with salespeople. Lead scoring and nurturing relies heavily on natural language generation (NLG) and natural-language processing (NLP) to help improve each lead's score.

Combining historical selling, pricing and buying data in a single machine learning model improves the accuracy and scale of sales forecasts. Factoring in differences inherent in every account given their previous history and product and service purchasing cycles is invaluable in accurately predicting their future buying levels. AI and machine learning algorithms integrated into CRM, sales management and sales planning applications can explain variations in forecasts, provided they have the data available. Forecasting demand for new products and services is an area where AI and machine learning are reducing the risk of investing in entirely new selling strategies for new products.

Knowing the propensity of a given customer to churn versus renew is invaluable in improving Customer Lifetime Value. Analyzing a diverse series of factors to see which customers are going to churn or leave versus those that will renew is among the most valuable insights AI and machine learning is delivering today. Being able to complete a Customer Lifetime Value Analysis for every customer a company has provides a prioritized roadmap of where the health of client relationships are excellent versus those that need attention. Many companies are using Customer Lifetime Value Analysis as a proxy for a customer health score that gets reviewed monthly.

Knowing the strategies, techniques and time management approaches the top 10% of salespeople to rely on to excel far beyond quota and scaling those practices across the sales team based on AI-driven insights. All sales managers and leaders think about this often, especially in sales teams where performance levels vary widely. Knowing the capabilities of the highest-achieving salespeople, then selectively recruiting those sales team candidates who have comparable capabilities delivers solid results. Leaders in the field of applying AI to talent management include Eightfold whose approach to talent management is refining recruiting and every phase of managing an employee's potential. Please see the recent New York Times feature of them here.

Guided Selling is progressing rapidly from a personalization-driven selling strategy to one that capitalized on data-driven insights, further revolutionizing sales. AI- and machine learning-based guided selling is based on prescriptive analytics that provides recommendations to salespeople of which products, services, and bundles to offer at which price. 62% of highest performing salespeople predict guided selling adoption will accelerate based on its ability rank potential opportunities by value and suggest next steps according to Salesforces' latest State of Sales research study.

Improving the sales team's productivity by using AI and machine learning to analyze the most effective actions and behaviors that lead to more closed sales. AI and machine learning-based sales contact and customer predictive analytics take into account all sources of contacts with customers and determine which are the most effective. Knowing which actions and behaviors are correlated with the highest close rates, sales managers can use these insights to scale their sales teams to higher performance.

Sales and marketing are better able to define a price optimization strategy using all available data analyzing using AI and machine learning algorithms. Pricing continues to be an area the majority of sales and marketing teams learn to do through trial and error. Being able to analyze pricing data, purchasing history, discounts are taken, promotional programs participated in and many other factors, AI and machine learning can calculate the price elasticity for a given customer, making an optimized price more achievable.

Personalizing sales and marketing content that moves prospects from MQLs to SQLs is continually improving thanks to AI and machine learning. Marketing Automation applications including HubSpot and many others have for years been able to define which content asset needs to be presented to a given prospect at a given time. What's changed is the interactive, personalized nature of the content itself. Combining analytics, personalization and machine learning, marketing automation applications are now able to tailor content and assets that move opportunities forward.

Solving the many challenges of sales engineering scheduling, sales enablement support and dedicating the greatest amount of time to the most high-value accounts is getting solved with machine learning. CRM applications including Salesforce can define a salesperson's schedule based on the value of the potential sale combined with the strength of the sales lead, based on its lead score. AI and machine learning optimize a salesperson's time so they can go from one customer meeting to the next, dedicating their time to the most valuable prospects.

HOW TO INCREASE SALES USING MACHINE LEARNING (CROSS-SELLING AND UP-SELLING)

The probability of selling a product to an existing customer is 60-70%, while for new customers it is only 5-20%. Quite logically, there are numerous strategies focused exactly on existing clients, and cross-selling and upselling are among them. If used effectively, they can increase your sales and, therefore, profits. And if backed with machine learning, cross-sell and upsell campaigns can significantly improve your business' position on the market. But why and how to use machine learning in the case of cross-selling and up-selling?

Cross-selling focuses on complementary products. For instance, if a customer buys a bicycle, they may also be interested in buying a helmet or knee pads. The McDonalds famous phrase "Would you like fries with that?" is a great example of cross-selling. It allows the company to sell more than 4 million kilograms of fries per day.

In turn, upselling is about reaching existing customers and offering them an opportunity to upgrade the product they have already purchased or to buy a more expensive item.

Now, when the difference is absolutely clear, it is time to tell you why to use machine learning to boost your sales. And what to do to reach such better results with using machine learning for cross-selling and up-selling.

1. Machine Learning is a key to personalized recommendations and improves cross-selling and up-selling opportunities

You have already collected more than enough data about your customers. You have data about your customers age, location, gender, hobbies, buying history, marital status etc. and even did customer segmentation for better offering. That's great, but machine learning algorithms can significantly improve your offer personalization. Thanks to data-driven recommendations, customers will get the right offers at the right time, and, therefore, purchase more products. Here is an example for you — Amazon identifies which items are often purchased together. After that shows for users potential complementary products. This trick ensures better customer experience. As users receive exactly those recommendations which they may be waiting for.

Machine learning algorithms are usually divided into two categories: collaborative filtering and content-based filtering. However, combining both of these approaches is also a popular way of building a recommender system. In case you are not familiar with these methods or feel not confident enough when using them, we highly recommend you to look for an expert. Otherwise, your real time product recommendation system may turn out to be not really efficient.

2. Machine Learning sharpens sales prediction

One of the best things about machine learning is that it never stops learning from new data. Sorry for a little tautology, but this ability allows forecasting your customers' behavior and expectations in the future. On the basis of historical and new data, a machine learning model can increase the accuracy of the sales forecast. This is especially important and useful when you need to predict how your customers will perceive new products or services. You will understand how to work on your cross-selling and upselling strategies, and reduce the risk of inefficient marketing.

Apart from this, using machine learning and customer predictive analytics, it is possible to identify the most effective sources of contacts with clients. Again, this can help you to polish your selling strategy and gain more profits.

3. Machine Learning makes dynamic pricing possible

Dynamic pricing is among the latest pricing trends — it implies continuous altering of product prices, in reaction to real time demand and supply. This model allows better control on the pricing strategy, gives flexibility without reducing the brand value, and saves budget over the long run. And, obviously, dynamic pricing can be a great help when you are cross-selling or upselling your products.

However, it is virtually impossible to efficiently monitor other items and follow the real time demand and supply manually, since there is too much data to check and analyze. But machine learning can solve the problem — a properly built model will take into account a lot of factors. It will take much more than you will be able to consider without such an algorithm, provide you with precise data, and ensure much faster responses to demand fluctuations.

4. Machine Learning is more efficient than automated A/B testing

A/B testing is also known as split testing — it is an experiment implying dividing the audience, testing a number of variations, and defining which of them works better than the others. For instance, the first group of customers receives a special upsell offer with a certain discount, while the second group gets the same offer, but with a different discount. Comparing the results and understanding which offer triggered more upsells, you will figure out the most efficient way to build your upselling campaign.

Sounds inspiring, but machine learning algorithms are much better than A/B testing — instead of focusing only on two options, they allow testing thousands of variations. Besides, A/B testing is a rather time-consuming process, but machine learning has no problem like this, so you and your team will be able to spend the time saved, for instance, on improving the selling strategy or working on new products. In this way, with machine learning methods, you will be able to bring your campaign to perfection in a very short time.

5. Machine Learning simplifies churn analysis and prediction

Making your business stable can be very challenging if you somehow forget about churn analysis. It refers to the customer attrition rate, and helps to define the reasons of churn. After that you could develop effective strategies for dealing with this issue.

Applying machine learning to churn models allows using much more variables than you could ever process manually. Besides, this trick may also expose those correlations and patterns which you would never notice on your own. And, logically, the results of churn analysis and prediction based on machine learning would be much more accurate than the ordinary ones. So, again, you will be able to build more efficient cross-selling and up-selling strategies.

WAYS TO USE DATA SCIENCE TO DRIVE YOUR CROSS-SELL AND UPSELL ACTIVITY

Getting more from what you have is the key tenet of the cross-selling and upselling mantra. By running deeper analysis on your customer information, you get more from your data. You then take these new insights and get more revenue from your existing customer-base by offering them relevant products and services. It's a win-win process, when it works.

Increasing customer lifetime value works for both the business and the customer. More revenue (with lower marketing spend) for the business and more relevancy and loyalty from the customer. Yet, achieving this sweet spot requires complex analysis of the customer, their actions and their needs.

Here are ways data science can help drive additional customer value:

Analyse & segment your customers

Before an analysis of customers for cross selling can be done, the dataset must first be divided into segments or cohorts, based along shared attributes, such as average spend, age, location or gender.

To successfully segment a dataset requires detailed data mining techniques to correctly decide how and where the segments should be created. Once created, cohort analysis enables the organisation not only to view which customers might buy more, but also to understand what the might buy, and when.

Understating these basic facts about your segments will allow you to begin to test and implement changes to increase any segment's value.

Modelling for uplift

One of the key goals in this analysis is to implement net lift modelling. This technique develops targeting or predictive analytics tools that not only identify who can spend more, but also the likelihood of whether they will do it or not.

Uplift modelling is a technique that uses a randomised scientific control to both measure the effectiveness of a marketing action and also to build a predictive model. This model predicts the incremental response to the marketing action.

Increase customer lifetime value and grow wallet share with predictive analytics.

Pick the next best product

Once a key audience has been identified for cross or upsell, a compelling offer must be selected. Next best product to recommend models are the foundation of cross-sell targeting analytics. These encompass triggers, segmentation, regression models and optimisation.Such models provide answers to the what (product), whom (customers), when (timing) and how (channel) of this exercise. Further consideration in the model also needs to be given to inter-purchase time, especially in retail.

Market Basket Analysis

Using historic analysis of customer data can highlight if a certain combination of products purchased makes an additional purchase more likely. This is called market basket analysis (also called as MBA). It is a widely used technique to identify the best possible mix of frequently bought products or services. This is also called product association analysis.

Basket

Association analysis is mostly done based on an algorithm named Apriori Algorithm. The Outcome of this analysis is called association rules and can be implemented into marketing activity to trigger upsell and cross-sell actions.

Combine forecasting with predictive analytics and decision optimisation to create insights and turn them into actions

Clustering

By using machine learning techniques, multivariate data can be mined and processed to identify groups of customers who display closely matched activities and traits. These commonalities to make them likely to behave in a similar fashion to one another when presented with an offer or incentive for increased spend.

Cluster analysis is not one particular algorithm but the general task that needs to be solved. The appropriate algorithm to use in each case depends on the individual dataset and intended use of the outcomes.

Deep Learning and Deep Neural Networks

Deep learning is a part of the wider area of machine learning. The main differentiator between the broader set of machine learning and deep learning is that deep learning applies a greater level of learning on the technology than some more task-specific techniques found in other areas of machine learning.

Deep learning removes more of the human element of cross-sell and upsell analysis and allows a system to learn and implement its own findings from the underlying data.

HOW TO HANDLE MISSING DATA IN MACHINE LEARNING

What is missing data? In simple terms, it's data where values are missing for some of the attributes. Now that we know how important it is to deal with missing data, let's look at five techniques to handle it correctly.

Missing values are representative of the messiness of real world data. There can be a multitude of reasons why they occur — ranging from human errors during data entry, incorrect sensor readings, to software bugs in the data processing pipeline.

The normal reaction is frustration. Missing data are probably the most widespread source of errors in your code, and the reason for most of the exception-handling. If you try to remove them, you might reduce the amount of data you have available dramatically — probably the worst that can happen in machine learning.

Types of Missing Data

Understanding the nature of missing data is critical in determining what treatments can be applied to overcome the lack of data. Data can be missing in the following ways:

Missing Completely At Random (MCAR): When missing values are randomly distributed across all observations, then we consider the data to be missing completely at random. A quick check for this is to compare two parts of data – one with missing observations and the other without missing observations. On a t-test, if we do not find any difference in means between the two samples of data, we can assume the data to be MCAR.

Missing At Random (MAR): The key difference between MCAR and MAR is that under MAR the data is not missing randomly across all observations, but is missing randomly only within sub-samples of data. For example, if high school GPA data is missing randomly across all schools in a district, that data will be considered MCAR. However, if data is randomly missing for students in specific schools of the district, then the data is MAR.

Not Missing At Random (NMAR): When the missing data has a structure to it, we cannot treat it as missing at random. In the above example, if the data was missing for all students from specific schools, then the data cannot be treated as MAR.

Mean Or Median Imputation

When data is missing at random, we can use list-wise or pair-wise deletion of the missing observations. However, there can be multiple reasons why this may not be the most feasible option:

There may not be enough observations with non-missing data to produce a reliable analysis

In predictive analytics, missing data can prevent the predictions for those observations which have missing data

External factors may require specific observations to be part of the analysis

In such cases, we impute values for missing data. A common technique is to use the mean or median of the non-missing observations. This can be useful in cases where the number of missing observations is low. However, for large number of missing values, using mean or median can result in loss of variation in data and it is better to use imputations. Depending upon the nature of the missing data, we use different techniques to impute data that have been described below.

Multivariate Imputation By Chained Equations (MICE)

MICE assumes that the missing data are Missing at Random (MAR). It imputes data on a variable-by-variable basis by specifying an imputation model per variable. MICE uses predictive mean matching (PMM) for continuous variables, logistic regressions for binary variables, bayesian polytomous regressions for factor variables, and proportional odds model for ordered variables to impute missing data.

To set up the data for MICE, it is important to note that the algorithm uses all the variables in the data for predictions. In this case, variables that may not be useful for predictions, like the ID variable, should be removed before implementing this algorithm.

Secondly, as mentioned above, the algorithm treats different variables differently. So, all categorical variables should be treated as factor variables before implementing MICE.

Random Forest

Random forest is a non-parametric imputation method applicable to various variable types that works well with both data missing at random and not missing at random. Random forest uses multiple decision trees to estimate missing values and outputs OOB (out of bag) imputation error estimates.

One caveat is that random forest works best with large datasets and using random forest on small datasets runs the risk of overfitting. The extent of overfitting leading to inaccurate imputations will depend upon how closely the distribution for predictor variables for non-missing data resembles the distribution of predictor variables for missing data. For example, if the distribution of race/ethnicity for non-missing data is similar to the distribution of race/ethnicity for missing data, overfitting is not likely to throw off results. However, if the two distributions differ, the accuracy of imputations will suffer.

The MICE library in R also allows imputations by random forest by setting the method to "rf". The authors of the MICE library have provided an example on how to implement the random forest method here.

To sum up data imputations is tricky and should be done with care. It is important to understand the nature of the data that is missing when deciding which algorithm to use for imputations. While using the above algorithms, predictor variables should be set up carefully to avoid confusion in the methods implemented during imputation. Finally, you can test the quality of your imputations by normalized root mean square error (NRMSE) for continuous variables and proportion of falsely classified (PFC) for categorical variables.

Deductive Imputation

This is an imputation rule defined by logical reasoning, as opposed to a statistical rule. For example, if someone has 2 children in year 1, year 2 has missing values, and 2 children in year 3, we can reasonably impute that they have 2 children in year 2. It requires no inference, and the true value can be assessed. But it can be time-consuming or might require specific coding.

Even though it's accurate, deductive imputation cannot be applied to all datasets. That's why we need to use statistical ways to impute the missing values in some cases.

Regression Imputation

This approach replaces missing values with a predicted value based on a regression line.

Regression is a statistical method which shows the relationship between a dependent variable and independent variables. It's expressed as $y = mx + b$ where m is the slope, b is a constant, x is the independent variable and y is the dependent variable.

Stochastic Regression Imputation

This aims to preserve the variability of data. To achieve this, we add an error (or residual term) to each predicted score. This residual term is normally distributed with a mean of zero and a variance equal to the variance of the predictor used for imputing.

Multiply-Stochastic Regression Imputation

This is similar to singly-stochastic regression imputation (i.e., where the missing values in a given column are replaced with the predicted values based on a regression line and random error), but it is done for a few iterations and the final value is just aggregated by the mean.

TOP SOURCES FOR MACHINE LEARNING DATASETS

It can be quite hard to find a specific dataset to use for a variety of machine learning problems or to even experiment on. The list below does not only contain great datasets for experimentation but also contains a description, usage examples and in some cases the algorithm code to solve the machine learning problem associated with that dataset.

1- Kaggle Datasets

Each dataset is a small community where you can have a discussion about data, find some public code or create your own projects in Kernels. They contain a numerous amount of real-life datasets of all shapes and sizes and in many different formats. You can also see "Kernels" associated with each dataset where many different data scientists have provided notebooks to analyze the dataset. Sometimes you can find notebooks with algorithms that solve the prediction problem in this specific dataset.

2- Amazon Datasets

Registry of Open Data on AWS

Unless specifically stated in the applicable dataset documentation, datasets available through the Registry of Open...

This source contains many datasets in different fields such as: (Public Transport, Ecological Resources, Satellite Images, etc.). It also has a search box to help you find the dataset you are looking for and it also has dataset description and Usage examples for all datasets which are very informative and easy to use!

The datasets are stored in Amazon Web Services (AWS) resources such as Amazon S3 — A highly scalable object storage service in the Cloud. If you are using AWS for machine learning experimentation and development, that will be handy as the transfer of the datasets will be very quick because it is local to the AWS network.

3- UCI Machine Learning Repository:

Another great repository of 100s of datasets from the University of California, School of Information and Computer Science. It classifies the datasets by the type of machine learning problem. You can find datasets for univariate and multivariate time-series datasets, classification, regression or recommendation systems. Some of the datasets at UCI are already cleaned and ready to be used.

4- Google's Datasets Search Engine:

In late 2018, Google did what they do best and launched another great service. It is a toolbox that can search for datasets by name. Their aim is to unify tens of thousands of different repositories for datasets and make that data discoverable. Well done, Google.

5- Microsoft Datasets:

In July 2018, Microsoft along with the external research community announced the launch of "Microsoft Research Open Data"

It contains a data repository in the cloud dedicated to facilitating collaboration across the global research community. It offers a bunch of curated datasets that were used in published research studies.

6- Awesome Public Datasets Collection:

This is a great source of datasets organized by topics, such as Biology, Economics, Education, etc. Most of the datasets listed there are free, but you should always check the licensing requirements before using any dataset.

7- Government Datasets:

It's also easy to find government-related datasets. Many countries have shared a variety of datasets to the public as an exercise of transparency. Here are some examples:

EU Open Data Portal: European Government Datasets.

US Gov Data

New Zealand's Government Dataset.

Indian Government Dataset.

Northern Ireland Public Dataset

8- Computer Vision Datasets:

If you are working on image processing, computer vision or deep learning then this should be your source of data for experiments.

Visual Data contains a handful number of great datasets that can be used to build computer vision (CV) models. You can look for a certain dataset by a certain CV subject such as Semantic Segmentation, Image captioning, Image Generation or even by the solution such as (Self-driving cars dataset).

ARTIFICIAL INTELLIGENCE (AI)

WHAT IS ARTIFICIAL INTELLIGENCE (AI)?

Artificial intelligence refers to the simulation of human intelligence in machines that are programmed to think like humans and mimic their actions. The term may also be applied to any machine that exhibits traits associated with a human mind such as learning and problem-solving.

The ideal characteristic of artificial intelligence is its ability to rationalize and take actions that have the best chance of achieving a specific goal.

When most people hear the term artificial intelligence, the first thing they usually think of is robots. That's because big-budget films and novels weave stories about human-like machines that wreak havoc on Earth. But nothing could be further from the truth.

Artificial intelligence is based on the principle that human intelligence can be defined in a way that a machine can easily mimic it and execute tasks, from the most simple to those that are even more complex. The goals of artificial intelligence include learning, reasoning, and perception.

As technology advances, previous benchmarks that defined artificial intelligence become outdated. For example, machines that calculate basic functions or recognize text through optimal character recognition are no longer considered to embody artificial intelligence, since this function is now taken for granted as an inherent computer function.

AI is continuously evolving to benefit many different industries. Machines are wired using a cross-disciplinary approach based in mathematics, computer science, linguistics, psychology, and more.

Algorithms often play a very important part in the structure of artificial intelligence, where simple algorithms are used in simple applications, while more complex ones help frame strong artificial intelligence.

Applications of AI

The applications for artificial intelligence are endless. The technology can be applied to many different sectors and industries. AI is being tested and used in the healthcare industry for dosing drugs and different treatment in patients, and for surgical procedures in the operating room.

Other examples of machines with artificial intelligence include computers that play chess and self-driving cars. Each of these machines must weigh the consequences of any action they take, as each action will impact the end result. In chess, the end result is winning the game. For self-driving cars, the computer system must account for all external data and compute it to act in a way that prevents a collision.

Artificial intelligence also has applications in the financial industry, where it is used to detect and flag activity in banking and finance such as unusual debit card usage and large account deposits—all of which help a bank's fraud department. Applications for AI are also being used to help streamline and make trading easier. This is done by making supply, demand, and pricing of securities easier to estimate.

Categorization of AI

Artificial intelligence can be divided into two different categories: weak and strong. Weak artificial intelligence embodies a system designed to carry out one particular job. Weak AI systems include video games such as the chess example from above and personal assistants such as Amazon's Alexa and Apple's Siri. You ask the assistant a question, it answers it for you.

Strong artificial intelligence systems are systems that carry on the tasks considered to be human-like. These tend to be more complex and complicated systems. They are programmed to handle situations in which they may be required to problem solve without having a person intervene. These kinds of systems can be found in applications like self-driving cars or in hospital operating rooms.

Since its beginning, artificial intelligence has come under scrutiny from scientists and the public alike. One common theme is the idea that machines will become so highly developed that humans will not be able to keep up and they will take off on their own, redesigning themselves at an exponential rate.

Another is that machines can hack into people's privacy and even be weaponized. Other arguments debate the ethics of artificial intelligence and whether intelligent systems such as robots should be treated with the same rights as humans.

Self-driving cars have been fairly controversial as their machines tend to be designed for the lowest possible risk and the least casualties. If presented with a scenario of colliding with one person or another at the same time, these cars would calculate the option that would cause the least amount of damage.

Another contentious issue many people have with artificial intelligence is how it may affect human employment. With many industries looking to automate certain jobs through the use of intelligent machinery, there is a concern that people would be pushed out of the workforce. Self-driving cars may remove the need for taxis and car-share programs, while manufacturers may easily replace human labor with machines, making people's skills more obsolete.

ARTIFICIAL INTELLIGENCE VS MACHINE LEARNING

Artificial intelligence and machines have become a part of everyday life, but that doesn't mean we understand them well. Do you know the difference between machine learning (ML) and artificial intelligence (AI)?

If you're hoping to use one or the other in your business, it's important to know which one to focus on. ML and AI are related, but they aren't the same, and they aren't necessarily suited to the same tasks. You can take your business to the next level by knowing when to choose ML or AI.

This guide will walk you through everything you need to know about AI and ML, from what they are to why they're different. Keep reading to learn how this modern tech can help you and your business.

AI means that machines can perform tasks in ways that are "intelligent." These machines aren't just programmed to do a single, repetitive motion -- they can do more by adapting to different situations.

Machine learning is technically a branch of AI, but it's more specific than the overall concept. Machine learning is based on the idea that we can build machines to process data and learn on their own, without our constant supervision.

Needless to say, AI and machine learning are relatively new. The concepts stretch back to certain imaginative individuals from decades, centuries and even millennia ago. But it's only recently that these dreams became realities.

The concept of AI really solidified with the earliest computers. These first computers weren't making any decisions on their own, of course. However, they were "logical machines" that were able to remember information and make calculations. The people creating these machines knew that they were working to make a brain-like machine.

However, technology has gotten much more advanced since then, so our ability to make brain-like machines has advanced, too. In the past few decades, we've also developed a better understanding of how our own brains actually work.

The more we understand these things, the more the approach to AI changes. Our computers can now make incredibly complex calculations, but developments don't really focus on those now. Instead, people are seeking to create machines that can make decisions in similar ways to humans and use those decisions to complete tasks.

DIFFERENCES BETWEEN AI AND MACHINE LEARNING

What is machine learning?

Machine learning (ML) is a branch of artificial intelligence, and as defined by Computer Scientist and machine learning pioneer Tom M. Mitchell: "Machine learning is the study of computer algorithms that allow computer programs to automatically improve through experience." ML it's one of the ways we expect to achieve AI. Machine learning relies on working with small to large data-sets, by examining and comparing the data to find common patterns and explore nuances.

For instance, if you provide a machine learning model with a lot of songs that you enjoy, along their corresponding audio statistics (dance-ability, instrumentality, tempo or genre), it will be able to automate (depending of the supervised machine learning model used) and generate a recommender system as to suggest you with music in the future that (with a high percentage of probability rate) you'll enjoy, similarly as to what Netflix, Spotify, and other companies do.

In a simple example, if you load a machine learning program with a considerable large data-set of x-ray pictures along with their description (symptoms, items to consider, etc.), it will have the capacity to assist (or perhaps automatize) the data analysis of x-ray pictures later on. The machine learning model will look at each one of the pictures in the diverse data-set, and find common patterns found in pictures that have been labeled with comparable indications. Furthermore, (assuming that we use a good ML algorithm for images) when you load the model with new pictures it will compare its parameters with the examples it has gathered before in order to disclose to you how likely the pictures contain any of the indications it has analyzed previously.

The type of machine learning from the previous example is called "supervised learning," where supervised learning algorithms try to model relationship and dependencies between the target prediction output and the input features, such that we can predict the output values for new data based on those relationships, which it has learned from previous data-sets fed.

Unsupervised learning, another type of machine learning are the family of machine learning algorithms, which are mainly used in pattern detection and descriptive modeling. These algorithms do not have output categories or labels on the data (the model is trained with unlabeled data).

Reinforcement Learning

Reinforcement learning, the third popular type of machine learning aims at using observations gathered from the interaction with its environment to take actions that would maximize the reward or minimize the risk. In this case, the reinforcement learning algorithm (called the agent) continuously learns from its environment using iteration. A great example of reinforcement learning are computers reaching super-human state and beating humans on computer games.

Machine learning is mesmerizing; particularly its advanced sub-branches, i.e. deep learning and the various types of neural networks. In any case, it is "magic" (Computational Learning Theory), regardless of whether the public at times has issues observing its internal workings. In fact, while some tend to compare deep learning and neural networks to the way the human brain works, there are important differences between the two.

What is Artificial Intelligence (AI)?

Artificial intelligence, on the other hand, is exceptionally wide in scope. "Artificial intelligence is the science and engineering of making computers behave in ways that, until recently, we thought required human intelligence."

That is a great way to define AI in a single sentence; however, it still shows how broad and vague the field is. Fifty years ago, a chess-playing program was considered a form of AI, since game theory, along with game strategies, were capabilities that only a human brain could perform. Nowadays, a Chess game would be considered dull and antiquated, due to the fact that it can be found on almost every computer's OS, therefore, "until recently" is something that progresses with time.

The term AI "is aspirational, a moving target based on those capabilities that humans possess but which machines do not." AI also includes a considerable measure of technology advances that we know. Machine learning is only one of them. Prior works of AI utilized different techniques, for instance, Deep Blue, the AI that defeated the world's chess champion in 1997, used a method called tree search algorithms to evaluate millions of moves at every turn.

AI as we know it today is symbolized with Human-AI interaction gadgets by Google Home, Siri and Alexa, by the machine learning powered video prediction systems that power Netflix, Amazon and YouTube. These technology advancements are progressively becoming important in our daily lives. In fact, they are intelligent assistants that enhance our abilities as humans, and professionals — making us more and more productive.

In contrast to machine learning, AI is a moving target, and its definition changes as its related technological advancements turn out to be further developed. Possibly, within a few decades, today's innovative AI advancements will be considered as dull as flip-phones are to us right now.

TOP AI FRAMEWORKS AND MACHINE LEARNING LIBRARIES

1. TensorFlow

"An open source machine learning framework for everyone"

TensorFlow is Google's open source AI framework for machine learning and high performance numerical computation.

TensorFlow is a Python library that invokes C++ to construct and execute dataflow graphs. It supports many classification and regression algorithms, and more generally, deep learning and neural networks.

One of the more popular AI libraries, TensorFlow services clients like AirBnB, eBay, Dropbox, and Coca-Cola.

Plus, being backed by Google has its perks. TensorFlow can be learned and used on Colaboratory, a Jupyter notebook environment that runs in the cloud, requires no set-up, and is designed to democratize machine learning education and research.

Some of TensorFlow's biggest benefits are its simplifications and abstractions, which keeps code lean and development efficient.

TensorFlow is AI framework designed to help everyone with machine learning.

2. Scikit-learn

Scikit-learn is an open source, commercially usable AI library. Another Python library, scikit-learn supports both supervised and unsupervised machine learning. Specifically, it supports classification, regression, and clustering algorithms, as well as dimensionality reduction, model selection, and preprocessing.

It's built on the NumPY, matplotlib, and SciPy libraries, and in fact, the name "scikit-learn" is a play on "SciPy Toolkit."

Scikit-learn markets itself as "simple and efficient tools for data mining and data analysis" that is "accessible to everybody, and reusable in various contexts."

To support these claims, scikit-learn offers an extensive user guide so that data scientists can quickly access resources on anything from multiclass and multilabel algorithms to covariance estimation.

AI as a Data Analyst

AI, and specifically machine learning, has advanced to a point where it can perform the day-to-day analysis that most business people require. Does this mean that data scientists and analysts should fear for their jobs?

We don't think so. With self-service analytics, machine learning algorithms can handle the reporting grunt work so that analysts and data scientists can focus their time on the advanced tasks that leverage their degrees and skillsets. Plus, business people won't need to wait around for the answers they need.

3. Theano

"A Python library that allows you to define, optimize, and evaluate mathematical expressions involving multi-dimensional arrays efficiently"

Theano is a Python library and optimizing compiler designed for manipulating and evaluating expressions. In particular, Theano evaluates matrix-valued expressions.

Speed is one of Theano's strongest suits. It can compete toe-to-toe with the speed of hand-crafted C language implementations that involve a lot of data. By taking advantage of recent GPUs, Theano has also been able to top C on a CPU by a significant degree.

By pairing elements of a computer algebra system (CAS) with elements of an optimizing compiler, Theano provides an ideal environment for tasks where complicated mathematical expressions require repeated, fast evaluation. It can minimize extraneous compilation and analysis while providing important symbolic features.

Even though new development has ceased for Theano, it's still a powerful and efficient platform for deep learning.

Theano is a machine learning library that can help you define and optimize mathematical expressions with ease.

4. Caffe

Caffe is an open deep learning framework developed by Berkeley AI Research in collaboration with community contributors, and it offers both models and worked examples for deep learning.

Caffe prioritizes expression, speed, and modularity in its framework. In fact, its architecture supports configuration-defined models and optimization without hard coding, as well as the ability to switch between CPU and GPU.

Plus, Caffe is highly adaptive to research experiments and industry deployments because it can process over 60M images per day with a single NVIDIA K40 GPU— one of the fastest convnet implementations available, according to Caffe.

Caffe's language is C++ and CUDA with Command line, Python, and MATLAB interfaces. Caffe's Berkeley Vision and Learning Center models are licensed for unrestricted use, and their Model Zoo offers an open collection of deep models designed to share innovation and research.

Caffe is an open deep learning framework and AI library developed by Berkeley.

5. Keras

Keras is a high-level neural network API that can run on top of TensorFlow, Microsoft Cognitive Toolkit, or Theano. This Python deep learning library facilitates fast experimentation and claims that "being able to go from idea to result with the least possible delay is key to doing good research."

Instead of an end-to-end machine learning framework, Keras operates as a user-friendly, easily extensible interface that supports modularity and total expressiveness. Standalone modules — such as neural layers, cost functions, and more — can be combined with few restrictions, and new modules are easy to add.

With consistent and simple APIs, user actions are minimized for common use cases. It can run in both CPU and GPU as well.

Keras is a python deep learning library that runs on top of other prominent machine learning libraries.

6. Microsoft Cognitive Toolkit

"A free, easy-to-use, open-source, commercial-grade toolkit that trains deep learning algorithms to learn like the human brain."

Previously known as Microsoft CNTK, Microsoft Cognitive Toolkit is an open source deep learning library designed to support robust, commercial-grade datasets and algorithms.

With big-name clients like Skype, Cortana, and Bing, Microsoft Cognitive Toolkit offers efficient scalability from a single CPU to GPUs to multiple machines— without sacrificing a quality degree of speed and accuracy.

Microsoft Cognitive Toolkit supports C++, Python, C#, and BrainScript. It offers pre-built algorithms for training, all of which can be customized, though you can use always use your own. Customization opportunities extend to parameters, algorithms, and networks.

Microsoft Cognitive Toolkit is a free and open source AI library that's designed to train deep learning algorithms like the human brain.

7. PyTorch

"An open source deep learning platform that provides a seamless path from research prototyping to production deployment."

PyTorch is an open source machine learning library for Python that was developed mainly by Facebook's AI research group.

PyTorch supports both CPU and GPU computations and offers scalable distributed training and performance optimization in research and production. It's two high-level features include tensor computation (similar to NumPy) with GPU acceleration and deep neural networks built on a tape-based autodiff system.

With extensive tools and libraries, PyTorch provides plenty of resources to support development, including:

AllenNLP, an open source research library designed to evaluate deep learning models for natural language processing.

ELF, a game research platform that allows developers to train and test algorithms in different game environments.

Glow, a machine learning compiler that enhances performance for deep learning frameworks on various hardware platforms.

PyTorch is a deep learning platform and AI library for research prototyping and production deployment.

8. Torch

Similar to PyTorch, Torch is a Tensor library that's similar to NumPy and also supports GPU (in fact, Torch proclaims that they put GPUs "first"). Unlike PyTorch, Torch is wrapped in LuaJIT, with an underlying C/CUDA implementation.

A scientific computing framework, Torch prioritizes speed, flexibility, and simplicity when it comes to building algorithms.

With popular neural networks and optimization libraries, Torch provides users with libraries that are easy to use while enabling flexible implementation of complex neural network topologies.

Torch is an AI framework for computing with LuaJIT.

TOP FRAMEWORKS FOR MACHINE LEARNING ENGINEERS

Machine learning engineers are part of the engineering team who build the product and the algorithms, making sure that it works reliably, quickly, and at-scale. They work closely with data scientist to understand the theoretical and business aspect of it. In the context of machine learning, the main summary of the differences is the following:

Machine learning engineers build, implement, and maintain production machine learning systems.

Data scientists conduct research to generate ideas about machine learning projects, and perform analysis to understand the metrics impact of machine learning systems.

Below is a list of frameworks for machine learning engineers:

Apache Singa is a general distributed deep learning platform for training big deep learning models over large datasets. It is designed with an intuitive programming model based on the layer abstraction. A variety of popular deep learning models are supported, namely feed-forward models including convolutional neural networks (CNN), energy models like restricted Boltzmann machine (RBM), and recurrent neural networks (RNN). Many built-in layers are provided for users.

Amazon Machine Learning is a service that makes it easy for developers of all skill levels to use machine learning technology. Amazon Machine Learning provides visualization tools and wizards that guide you through the process of creating machine learning (ML) models without having to learn complex ML algorithms and technology. It connects to data stored in Amazon S3, Redshift, or RDS, and can run binary classification, multiclass categorization, or regression on said data to create a model.

Azure ML Studio allows Microsoft Azure users to create and train models, then turn them into APIs that can be consumed by other services. Users get up to 10GB of storage per account for model data, although you can also connect your own Azure storage to the service for larger models. A wide range of algorithms are available, courtesy of both Microsoft and third parties. You don't even need an account to try out the service; you can log in anonymously and use Azure ML Studio for up to eight hours.

Caffe is a deep learning framework made with expression, speed, and modularity in mind. It is developed by the Berkeley Vision and Learning Center (BVLC) and by community contributors. Yangqing Jia created the project during his PhD at UC Berkeley. Caffe is released under the BSD 2-Clause license. Models and optimization are defined by configuration without hard-coding & user can switch between CPU and GPU. Speed makes Caffe perfect for research experiments and industry deployment. Caffe can process over 60M images per day with a single NVIDIA K40 GPU.

H2O makes it possible for anyone to easily apply math and predictive analytics to solve today's most challenging business problems. It intelligently combines unique features not currently found in other machine learning platforms including: Best of Breed Open Source Technology, Easy-to-use WebUI and

Familiar Interfaces, Data Agnostic Support for all Common Database and File Types. With H2O, you can work with your existing languages and tools. Further, you can extend the platform seamlessly into your Hadoop environments.

Massive Online Analysis (MOA) is the most popular open source framework for data stream mining, with a very active growing community. It includes a collection of machine learning algorithms (classification, regression, clustering, outlier detection, concept drift detection and recommender systems) and tools for evaluation. Related to the WEKA project, MOA is also written in Java, while scaling to more demanding problems.

MLlib (Spark) is Apache Spark's machine learning library. Its goal is to make practical machine learning scalable and easy. It consists of common learning algorithms and utilities, including classification, regression, clustering, collaborative filtering, dimensionality reduction, as well as lower-level optimization primitives and higher-level pipeline APIs.

mlpack, a C++-based machine learning library originally rolled out in 2011 and designed for "scalability, speed, and ease-of-use," according to the library's creators. Implementing mlpack can be done through a cache of command-line executables for quick-and-dirty, "black box" operations, or with a C++ API for more sophisticated work. Mlpack provides these algorithms as simple command-line programs and C++ classes which can then be integrated into larger-scale machine learning solutions.

Pattern is a web mining module for the Python programming language. It has tools for data mining (Google, Twitter and Wikipedia API, a web crawler, a

HTML DOM parser), natural language processing (part-of-speech taggers, n-gram search, sentiment analysis, WordNet), machine learning (vector space model, clustering, SVM), network analysis and <canvas> visualization.

Scikit-Learn leverages Python's breadth by building on top of several existing Python packages — NumPy, SciPy, and matplotlib — for math and science work. The resulting libraries can be used either for interactive "workbench" applications or be embedded into other software and reused. The kit is available under a BSD license, so it's fully open and reusable. Scikit-learn includes tools for many of the standard machine-learning tasks (such as clustering, classification, regression, etc.). And since scikit-learn is developed by a large community of developers and machine-learning experts, promising new techniques tend to be included in fairly short order.

Shogun is among the oldest, most venerable of machine learning libraries, Shogun was created in 1999 and written in C++, but isn't limited to working in C++. Thanks to the SWIG library, Shogun can be used transparently in such languages and environments: as Java, Python, C#, Ruby, R, Lua, Octave, and Matlab. Shogun is designed for unified large-scale learning for a broad range of feature types and learning settings, like classification, regression, or explorative data analysis.

TensorFlow is an open source software library for numerical computation using data flow graphs. TensorFlow implements what are called data flow graphs, where batches of data ("tensors") can be processed by a series of algorithms described by a graph. The movements of the data through the system are called "flows" — hence, the name. Graphs can be assembled with C++ or Python and can be processed on CPUs or GPUs.

Theano is a Python library that lets you to define, optimize, and evaluate mathematical expressions, especially ones with multi-dimensional arrays (numpy.ndarray). Using Theano it is possible to attain speeds rivaling hand-crafted C implementations for problems involving large amounts of data. It was written at the LISA lab to support rapid development of efficient machine learning algorithms. Theano is named after the Greek mathematician, who may have been Pythagoras' wife. Theano is released under a BSD license.

Torch is a scientific computing framework with wide support for machine learning algorithms that puts GPUs first. It is easy to use and efficient, thanks to an easy and fast scripting language, LuaJIT, and an underlying C/CUDA implementation. The goal of Torch is to have maximum flexibility and speed in building your scientific algorithms while making the process extremely simple. Torch comes with a large ecosystem of community-driven packages in machine learning, computer vision, signal processing, parallel processing, image, video, audio and networking among others, and builds on top of the Lua community.

Veles is a distributed platform for deep-learning applications, and it's written in C++, although it uses Python to perform automation and coordination between nodes. Datasets can be analyzed and automatically normalized before being fed to the cluster, and a REST API allows the trained model to be used in production immediately. It focuses on performance and flexibility. It has little hard-coded entities and enables training of all the widely recognized topologies, such as fully connected nets, convolutional nets, recurrent nets etc.

THE LIMITATIONS OF MACHINE LEARNING

Machine learning is one of the newest technologies that is poised to make significant changes in the way companies conduct their business. Machine learning refers to computer technology that relays intelligent output based on algorithmic decisions made after processing a user's input.

While still in its infancy, machine learning has already started being rolled out to consumers through different applications, such as Apple's Siri, Amazon's Alexa, and Microsoft's Cortana, among others. Apart from voice, the technology is used to process image data (e.g. Facebook's facial recognition technology) and text data (e.g. Google's machine-assisted language translation).

i) Quality issues

Quality is one of the biggest challenges for machine translation. Context is an important component of understanding a language. Unfortunately, no computer software can process the context of a language, which is critical for accurate translation.

Words can have different meanings in different languages. A computer program does not understand context, especially in complex situations, and cannot come up with an accurate translation of the meaning.

ii) Lack of feedback

Alexa and Siri do a good job of impersonating self-thinking intelligence software. However, in reality, they are not self-thinking, and have many problems when interacting with the end user. The same applies to the various translation software programs available on the market.

For example, when you want to launch a product or service in a foreign market, you will not be able to collaborate or get feedback from the software on the best way to convey your message to your target audience. In the best case scenario, using software to translate content for a new market would be a gamble.

iii) Lack of creativity

Mastering a language requires thousands of hours of exposure and practice. Some subject matter can be translated decently through machine intelligence. However, the translation software cannot master the language, which requires a lot of creativity.

Your language has to be creative to drive the point home either to your target audience or clients in foreign markets. Only a human translator that understands the foreign market can help you come up with creative ways of conveying your message through content.

iv) Lack of sensitivity

The culture of a country is partly reflected through its language(s). The values and norms of a country determine how people communicate with each other. Without having background knowledge and experience with the culture, it is impossible to know the meaning conveyed by specific words in the culture.

Machine programs do not understand a people's cultural values and norms. As a result, relying entirely on machine translation can lead to you delivering the wrong message to your customers. Even worse, some machine-translated words may end up being offensive to customers in a foreign market.

Businesses can get their content translated at a low cost by utilizing machine translation. However, the technology is often not the best solution. To get your content translated accurately, consider hiring a professional translation firm with expert multi-lingual staff that speaks the language of your target foreign markets.

www.ingramcontent.com/pod-product-compliance
Lightning Source LLC
Chambersburg PA
CBHW031217050326
40689CB00009B/1366